What Does Eating Disorder Recovery Look Like?

What Does Eating Disorder Recovery Look Like?

*Answers to Your Questions
about Therapy and Recovery*

Lucia Giombini
and Sophie Nesbitt

Foreword by Cara Lisette

Jessica Kingsley Publishers
London and Philadelphia

First published in Great Britain in 2023 by Jessica Kingsley Publishers
An imprint of John Murray Press

1

Disclaimer: The information contained in this book is not intended
to replace the services of trained medical professionals or to be a
substitute for medical advice. You are advised to consult a doctor
on any matters relating to your health, and in particular on any
matters that may require diagnosis or medical attention.

A CIP catalogue record for this title is available from the
British Library and the Library of Congress

ISBN 978 1 83997 220 1
eISBN 978 1 83997 219 5

Printed and bound in Great Britain by CPI Group

Jessica Kingsley Publishers' policy is to use papers that are natural,
renewable and recyclable products and made from wood grown in
sustainable forests. The logging and manufacturing processes are expected
to conform to the environmental regulations of the country of origin.

Jessica Kingsley Publishers
Carmelite House
50 Victoria Embankment
London EC4Y 0DZ

www.jkp.com

John Murray Press
Part of Hodder & Stoughton Limited
An Hachette UK Company

Contents

Foreword

The experience of living with an eating disorder can be chaotic and confusing. No matter whether you are new into your journey or have been struggling for a while, there will always be things that feel like they don't make sense, or that you can't quite find an answer to.

This isn't just true of the person experiencing the eating disorder, but also of their wider support network, including families, friends and, at times, professionals. It's also likely that each of those groups of people will have their own questions, which are different from each other and can be difficult to articulate.

One of the most challenging parts of living with an eating disorder is the impact it has on people's ability to communicate effectively. When your thoughts are consumed by food, and your body and your emotions numbed by your eating disorder, it can be incredibly difficult to have rational and calm conversations with others. Equally, if you're watching on as your loved one becomes increasingly unwell, that too will impact on your ability to share ideas and ask questions in a way that feels pragmatic and safe. Often, we have questions swirling around that we want to ask each other, but aren't in a place where we can have conversations that aren't entirely eating disorder driven and emotionally charged.

For many people, experiencing an eating disorder is an isolating and lonely experience. It feels like nobody understands and that you are the only person in the world who has ever felt so terrible. Maybe other people can recover, but you can't, because your eating disorder is different. Maybe other people can go on to live full and happy lives, but you won't, because your eating disorder feels more powerful than you can ever imagine. I know this, because I have been there. My anorexia, too, felt unique, different and inescapable, and it took me a long time to find out that it wasn't, and that I could recover too.

There were many parts of my journey through treatment and recovery where I felt unsure of what to expect and what was coming next. *What Does Eating Disorder Recovery Look Like? Answers to Your Questions about Therapy and Recovery* is exactly the kind of resource that would have benefited not only me, but my family too. The authors take you through the early stages of learning just what an eating disorder is and how it can impact somebody's life physically, behaviourally and psychologically, all the way up to thinking about how to plan for relapse prevention and moving on from treatment and therapy. There are answers to all sorts of questions that both people with eating disorders and their families might have, including around body image, treatment and food itself. In particular, the focus on the various psychological therapies for eating disorders is valuable, as the start of somebody's treatment journey can be a very confusing and frightening time. It's reassuring to learn that there are different options for therapy, and also why and how they can be effective; having hope that there is evidence-based support that can have such a significant impact on recovery is such an important part of the process. I truly think this book will be an invaluable resource for people at all different stages of their journey.

My own experiences of psychological therapy for my eating disorder have been invaluable, and undoubtedly are the reason I am so stable and engaged in recovery. Since my initial diagnosis I have received cognitive behavioural therapy, psychodynamic psychotherapy and therapeutic groups in inpatient and day patient services. Having such a wide range of support enabled me to learn so much about myself and my eating disorder, and truly my biggest piece of advice for anybody going through this process is to allow your therapist in and let them fight your eating disorder alongside you.

I hope that people will come away from reading this book with not only a clearer understanding of their own or their loved one's difficulties, but also with a renewed hope for recovery. Recovery is possible, and for me, learning more about my eating disorder and myself were key factors in making that happen.

Cara Lisette

Eating disorder campaigner, blogger and author of *The Eating Disorder Recovery Journal*

Acknowledgements

We would like to thank all the people and their families who worked with us and were brave enough to ask for help, and responded to our letters with such kindness and honesty. Their experiences and reflections have formed the basis of much of this book and we hope that makes the book feel authentic. We would like to thank all the young people at Rhodes Wood Hospital, Elysium Healthcare and the Psychological Therapy Team where we have both worked as clinicians. The lovely people we have met and the experience gained has also contributed much to our thinking. Also, Elysium Healthcare, in particular Joy Chamberlain, Quazi Haque, Lesley Collins and Vincent Cheung, who have fully invested in all aspects of our research and writing with complete belief that these projects are worthy and possible. Finally, we would like to thank Ellie Warwick for her invaluable editing and proof reading. We thank her for her time and patience.

Chapter 1

Why This Book?

Why and how we have written this book

Working in healthcare as clinical psychologists, we have been fortunate enough to work within many different types of services for people with eating disorders, some in hospital settings, and some in more community-based settings. We have also undertaken research to try to understand what helps with their difficulties and what our role as clinical psychologists is within the treatment process.

Over time we have observed a move away from healthcare providing structured services, to more personalized, individual approaches actively empowering the person with the eating disorder and their family in their own care. The development of service user involvement, which effectively means asking, listening to and responding to the views of people and their families about their care, has led to the idea of co-production. 'Co-production' is the term used to describe the collaboration between healthcare professionals and people receiving care, which has led to the acceptance and valuing of the view of the person and their families involved in their care. Whilst you may be wondering why this is relevant, this philosophy is very important to us, as it has led us to engage with people with eating disorders in such a way that we have been allowed into their worlds – your worlds. Through open and honest conversations, we have come to understand more about your pain and suffering in relation to the difficulties you and your families may experience as part of your illness and your recovery journey.

We have written this book for everyone who has ever wondered and feared: Why me? Why my family? Can I ever get better? And can things ever change? We do not assume we can answer all of these questions. However, we hope that by sharing the understanding of people who have battled an eating disorder, we can help you and your family currently struggling on that journey.

When considering writing this book we wanted it to represent what we have learnt from all the people with eating disorders and their families. When writing, we imagined that those people and their families would be our readers. In the true spirit of 'co-production' we had the idea of writing to the people we have worked with and their families and asking them to share their thoughts on unanswered questions, or questions they were too scared to ask. We were uncertain about how they might feel about this, and whether this was the best approach; however, we felt that it was the only way to allow that voice to be heard and valued through our writing.

Fortunately, we were met with a sea of support and interest in this idea, validating our own thoughts about the process. We used each and every letter we received to form the basis of our writing, in the hope that the themes and experiences discussed are authentic in their relation to those people and families who have been so kind and generous to share their personal experiences of the illness. When you are reading this book, you may notice different writing styles – sometimes we present psychological ideas and attempt to demystify them for you; other times we draw on examples of conversations we have had during the work we have undertaken, and use those conversations to help you to understand what we are trying to say. We decided to keep these differences to represent the different voices of the people we have encountered, and also of our own voices, with the hope that the integration of different perspectives can be helpful to you, the reader, and the people around you.

Our letter

Here is a copy of the letter we sent out to the people we have worked with and their families – we are sharing this here so you can feel part of the same co-production process. All the thoughts and reflections that this book may provoke in you will help people around you, and clinicians you might be working with, and may help to contribute to the improvement of a shared understanding.

Dear ...,

We trust you are well when reading this letter. We wanted to share an idea with you about a new book and we wondered if you would be kind enough to consider a request that may be helpful in terms of developing this idea. We have just completed a book on eating disorders which was created for professionals working in this area. Whilst we enjoyed writing this book, we are keen to work together again on a book that can reach many more of the people we have spent our lives working with – young people, adults and their families. These are the people that we really want to write the next book for.

As you will know, there is so much information out there – numerous books, articles and websites. However, we would like to contribute to making helpful information even more accessible. To do this we believe that we need to write together with the young people, adults and their families we meet in the therapy room.

Therefore, we are keen to find out about the questions you might have wanted to ask but couldn't, the questions that you asked that weren't answered and the questions that you asked where the answers may have helped or where the answers didn't help. We also appreciate that not all the questions get answered and may never be – we would be interested on your thoughts on those. We are aware that you have read books and looked at websites and you are very knowledgeable in this area, but we are sure that many times, particularly in difficult moments, you may still have questions, or you may be able to think back to the very early questions that you had. They can be related to specific aspects of the eating disorder, its origin and development, and/or the process of therapy, or anything else that comes into your mind regarding psychological disorders and well-being.

We are sending this letter to some of the people we are currently working with. We will collect all your questions and attempt some answers and reflections that we hope will help other people as well. Maybe the ones who are still struggling to ask for help or had a difficult experience of therapy. This dialogue will shape our book.

To reassure you, everything will be completely confidential, nothing personal will be disclosed and we will write and integrate things in such a way that nothing will feel revealing. We hope that by integrating a vast wealth of stories and ideas we will be able to create something that is appreciated by young people, adults and their families who are experiencing an eating disorder and who at times feel alienated in a world that talks about the complexity of eating disorders and their symptoms.

We wondered if you would be kind enough to write here the questions (as few or as many as you want) you had, and/or continue to have.

Your questions...

We hope that we can find the answers with you in our continued clinical work, but we also hope that the experience of the work we have done together will help many other people and their families who are experiencing the pain and anguish of an eating difficulty.

Thank you for the time you have taken to read this letter and we look forward to hearing from you.

With warmest wishes

Yours faithfully,

Lucia and Sophie

To date, most of the research on eating disorders has adopted a biological and medical approach which focuses on the reasons why eating disorders may develop, the different clinical features of the illness, and how treatment can positively impact on symptoms and the overall outcome for the person experiencing the eating disorder. This has been done at the expense of trying to understand more about the psychological experience of each individual who needs help. This is what we felt it was important to focus on in this book.

Within this book we are attempting, in fact, to reflect on the therapeutic conversations we had with many young people and adults who came to us for psychological therapy, and to address some of the many questions that they asked from the very first moment they contacted us. By talking about the main themes that people share with us in their therapy sessions, we hope to highlight the many different layers within these difficulties. We hope that these open and honest reflections can be helpful to you as the reader.

When an illness breaks our pathway through life, we tend to lose our way, and sometimes the meaning of life and our own identities can be lost or fractured. Coming to terms with this can be difficult, and we need to develop new stories that can be adapted to our different pathways and provide us with new meaning. Each time we tell our story we extract parts from our experience and add emotions and knowledge we gained after the event, and thus memory is not about simply reproducing a past event but about using the past to recreate, in the present, something new. Therapy supports people in this process. The different scientific models that have been suggested to describe eating disorders do not always capture the emotional issues that can lie beneath the symptoms. To better understand the emotion, we need to look beyond the scientific models and think more about the person's experience and help you, and your families, make sense of that.

The themes and questions we address in this book are the ones shared with the people we have met in the therapy room. We have listened to many stories of despair, anger, rejection, sadness and hope. We have offered comfort, looked for explanations and worked with these people, supporting them to make positive changes. Through the therapy experience we worked together to create a safe place, a middle area between the internal and the external world, in which we can explore personal experiences and the meaning of difficulties. All this work is to support the person we are working with to develop a new trustworthy relationship with both their external and internal world.

We see a psychological symptom as a warning sign, or like a red flag that flies up when something is asking us to respond to our inner needs. Of course, that symptom has a literal meaning, which may require a prompt and pragmatic medical and psychological response and careful management. However, it also has a more profound meaning, within the cultural, historical, social and psychological context of the person affected by it.

At the beginning of therapy, when you and your families start your journey towards recovery, everything seems confused. Usually, though, three key phases can be identified, the first being the acute phase of the disorder, which can feel very chaotic and at times scary and uncertain. The second phase is perhaps the moment when you realize that you need help and, finally, the third phase is when recovery efforts begin. During this time, you gradually come to the realization that you are finding small solutions to each part of your difficulties; alongside this you may be developing a new sense of self. It is a complicated, difficult and long process; some days go well, other days less so, but with the right help it is possible that you can recover.

Chapter 2

What Are Eating Disorders?

I n this chapter we tell you about the main eating disorders, based on the criteria of the diagnostic and classification systems that are commonly used in healthcare settings across the world. We will also tell you about the different recommended treatments according to the international guidelines. We appreciate that we are going to provide some technical information in this chapter which might feel tiresome to read, but we hope that this can help you to better understand what is provided by the healthcare system. We briefly touch upon the impact that the COVID-19 pandemic has had on the development and treatment of eating disorders. Holding in mind that whilst firm conclusions cannot be drawn at the time of writing, as we are still coping with the aftermath of the pandemic, we do know already that COVID-19 has had a profound impact. If at any point in your recovery you access services then its impact may still be felt, so we feel it is relevant to your experience. We then share our thoughts on the limits of diagnostic criteria and therapy based on specific guidelines ('manualized therapy'), and how approaches can be improved with the integration of a more personalized treatment that considers the meaning and emotion underlying the eating disorder symptoms. This can be used to shape the treatment and the recovery journey together with patients and families.

Eating disorders are difficult to understand

It is a highly regarded view that eating disorders are very difficult to understand, the consensus being that to reject food or to overconsume and purge to the point of severe physical risk is a bizarre and unfathomable idea. For many cultures where food is associated with prosperity, the rejection of food is often misunderstood. For other cultures, being selective about one's food is accepted and highly valued. One thing is clear from the different cultural perspectives: through history and in our lives, there is a complex relationship between eating, food, emotion and how we see our body. Whether we are battling against an eating disorder, or caring for or working alongside a person with an eating disorder, there is absolutely no question that eating disorders create many challenges to our thinking and understanding.

To help you to relate to these issues, regardless of whether you have ever experienced an eating disorder, we ask you now to take a few moments in quiet reflection to consider your own experience of life and the relationship you have had with your body and eating. For some, this might be a fleeting moment as for the best part you have generally felt content. However, we would ask these questions: Have you at some point felt uncomfortable naked? Have you ever felt uncomfortable or concerned about being overweight? Perhaps you may have wished you looked different in some way, or perhaps you have felt distress or pain at the way you feel you are being perceived. Other questions we would ask are related to your thoughts and experience of eating: Have you ever been on a diet and started thinking about food a lot throughout the day? Have you ever felt guilty about something you ate, or compared what you were eating to what other people were eating?

For some, these questions may have created an emotional turmoil, a realization that, yes, you have felt that way at some point. Perhaps for those for whom it was a fleeting experience, it may have been managed and adjusted to, but for others it may have been more long lasting, or may have initiated change in the way you thought about and managed food and seen and experienced your body. However, if you were able to relate to any aspect of these questions, then you will have entered some sense of understanding of what an eating disorder can create within an individual, and you may have some capacity to empathize with young people and adults who suffer from eating disorders.

If, however, you are living with an eating disorder, you will be in pain and distress, and you may feel this day after day. It may be driven by a deep and wholehearted belief that you are ugly, loathsome, bloated and distended. For some, it may be mild and only create a background noise in your emotional life. However, if your eating disorder is malignant, you will be experiencing an intense, unrelenting, tortured self-concern that renders life unliveable without the most intensive support from those around you. If you are enduring starvation or extreme binge-purging behaviours, you may also be experiencing thoughts of self-harm, depression and anxiety, as these difficulties can run hand in hand with eating disorders.[1] You may also be experiencing seriously delayed growth, brain blood-flow shutdown, osteoporosis (sometimes permanently damaged bones), infertility and unstable heart beats. Over long periods of time, starvation can lead to debilitating physical disabilities with the most serious of consequences, possibly resulting in multi-organ failure and death.

You may feel that your eating disorder has crippled your ability to get through to the world around you; you may feel 'locked in' emotionally. Simultaneously, you may also feel 'locked out' emotionally, as you may find it difficult to understand how those around you continue to love and support you. The eating disorder that is currently your company may have become a replacement for emotional communication. You may be struggling with expressing and receiving what matters most – your own feelings and the feelings of others. You will have no shortage of feelings, no poverty of emotion and no emptiness of real intentions or motivation, but feelings may seem to be segregated from words. Emotions may not be expressed and remain all too often disconnected from the tears and choreography of your facial movements. You may not cry in the way you used to, and might not express heightened emotion of any kind. This conflict may be masked by an expressionless, seemingly unconcerned face. The usual desires, thoughts and driving forces within you may feel captured and held hostage by weight and shape, and relentless ritualized eating behaviours. Your body has become the emotional experience. The world of eating disorders is a prison tightly bound by walls of distress at every turn.

You may already have had a longstanding difficulty

with eating and the way you feel about your body. This may have been a secret issue that you have shared with no one, creating a powerful sense of isolation and loneliness. Or you may have been able to acknowledge this at some level; you may have been to healthcare services and been further misunderstood, or received treatment that was positive, or perhaps negative. You may be in recovery and on a positive journey with managing your difficulties. For some, reading on may feel too confronting, but please do bear with us – there may be something in our writing that connects somewhere to your experience, and we do hope that is the case.

You may be a family member or carer of someone struggling. We warmly welcome you to our book as well, in the hope there will be something here for you too. There may also be readers who do not fall into any of the descriptions outlined above. We do not seek to categorize; we prefer to invite everyone with some form of struggle to share in the book in the hope that it can be helpful. This book is written with many people in mind, and all are warmly welcomed. We invite you as the reader to explore the contents of these chapters with the hope that some parts of it may help you or the people close to you in some way.

What are eating disorders?

Eating disorders are disturbances in eating behaviour and in the way you think and feel about food and your body. They can result in severe physical, emotional and social consequences that limit a person's ability to lead a happy and fulfilling life. If you are experiencing an eating disorder, you may be feeling very isolated and lonely. You may be keeping your behaviours a secret as you may feel ashamed and embarrassed about what you are doing or how you are feeling. You may also feel that you may be judged by others. Those who experience an eating disorder can find it a very lonely and isolating experience. Sometimes the eating disorder may be creating a sense of control; it may create feelings of power and strength. However, this is at odds with what it is actually doing, and you may experience the contradiction of knowing what you are doing and that it is not healthy for you.

At one level eating disorders seem to be mental health conditions that relate to food, weight and eating. However, the reality is that there are many factors that contribute to the development of an eating disorder, such as biological factors, environmental stressors and psychological/emotional patterns that lie underneath the visible symptoms. Certain social values, such as the overinvestment in appearance, consumerism, achievement and performance, contribute to shaping the way the eating disorder manifests, but they do not cause it. In the same way, a personal traumatic experience can represent a trigger for the development of an eating disorder, but it does not constitute a single cause. It is always in the conversation between individual and social needs that we can understand how psychological symptoms truly develop.

In eating disorders, there is often a very strong drive that may be telling you to restrict and control, paired with a very strong desire to eat. When we see restrictive eating patterns, we consider that you may be feeling scared of losing control over food and eating too much. We could say that anorexia nervosa includes in itself a virtual bulimic dimension. And vice versa: bulimia or binge eating behaviours are also characterized by persistent restrictive thinking.

Sometimes the worries and eating behaviours express the difficulty experienced when dealing with challenging situations in life such as school or work pressures, difficult friendships or relationships, losses and changes to life, which can create very overwhelming emotions. The eating disorder can also be linked to the experience of not feeling in tune with the surrounding environment. This may result in you feeling like you are on the outside or that you are different from others and that you don't fit in. This experience may make you want to withdraw from the world, shrinking emotionally and physically or transforming your body into a shield.

Eating disorders can have a devastating impact on your life, particularly on your mental health. They can create a distorted body image, obsessive thoughts about food, low self-esteem, mood swings, overwhelming guilt, anxiety and depression. An eating disorder may at times drive you to engage in excessive and compulsive exercise, even when your body is exhausted. They can also impact socially, leaving you feeling very isolated and lonely.

Different types of eating disorders

There are many different types of eating disorders, as defined in the *Diagnostic and Statistical Manual of Mental Disorders: DSM-5*, which is written by the American Psychiatric Association.[2] This manual was last updated in 2013; definitions are occasionally added or changed to take into account the changes in the presentation of illness that clinicians report. As with many different illnesses, eating disorders and the way they present can and have changed over time. One feature that is consistent across all the different eating disorders is the persistent dysregulation of eating or eating-related behaviour which leads to a change in the person's relationship with food and can affect both physical and psychological health.

If you are involved in treatment with a healthcare service, it is important that you are familiar with the DSM-5, because if you receive a formal diagnosis, it will be based on information taken from this manual. At the same time, it is also important to hold in mind the psychological impact that any diagnostic label may have on you, as this can be different for different people depending on their experience of the world. For some, this experience may feel reassuring as it gives your collection of difficulties a name, but for others this experience may feel stigmatizing, or make you feel not as heard, as your experience may not fit with the diagnostic system. A considerable number of people with eating disorders reported that they were told they were not meeting certain criteria and therefore could not be provided with help. They interpreted this as meaning that they were not ill enough, which caused a deterioration in their condition. We feel it is important to acknowledge the limitations of the diagnostic manual and the restricted resources that the healthcare system can provide.

We will now go on to describe the different eating disorders. These definitions are not taken directly from the DSM-5, but are rewritten in our own words to make them more easily understood.

+ **Anorexia nervosa:** This is where you persistently restrict your food intake. You will be losing weight or maintaining a very low body weight for your height.

You may be experiencing lots of issues with your body image and be very scared of gaining weight to the point where eating has become really hard and very scary. This can lead you at times to eat very little, and get rid of the food afterwards through purging or doing an excessive amount of exercise.

* **Bulimia nervosa:** You may be experiencing episodes of loss of control around food and eating, resulting in eating lots of food in a small amount of time. This is called binge eating. Often after a binge you may experience intense feelings of regret and try to make yourself sick, take laxatives to try to empty yourself of the food, or engage in other forms of behaviour to compensate such as overexercising.

* **Binge eating disorder:** You may be overeating very frequently, with no other behaviours to compensate. These phases of overeating are very common and run alongside feelings of being very out of control around food. You may be experiencing great distress and body image issues because of this.

There are two other groups of eating disorders we would like to mention to you. The first group is known as EDNOS, which stands for 'eating disorders not otherwise specified'. It can be rather confusing to understand, but it is helpful to know if this is how your difficulties are being talked about. If this term has been used to describe your difficulty, it basically means that you have some of the difficulties associated with some of the criteria, but not all of them. Please understand, some of the symptoms can be just as serious and debilitating; it is not a lesser diagnosis at all.

The second group that is important to mention is eating disorders that fall under the umbrella of ARFID. ARFID stands for 'avoidant restrictive food intake disorder'. In the past, these difficulties were talked about more informally as feeding disorders, but more recently the classification system for understanding these disorders has changed. If this term has been used to describe your difficulties you may be suffering from a sudden anxiety relating to eating – perhaps you are scared of choking or being sick when you eat. This can become very serious if the difficulties persist, as it can result in a decline in your physical well-being. In childhood and adolescence this can impact on your growth, and in adulthood on your general physical health.

Also, any illness that causes pain after eating can be very difficult to manage. For example, people with food allergies or gluten intolerance, where eating certain foods has caused discomfort or pain, can develop anxiety associated with eating those foods. This group of individuals can be very vulnerable to restrictive diets and weight loss. As yet this isn't represented in the research studies, so this is just our clinical impression based on some of the stories that you have told us. However, it is important that you get help to try and understand why this has happened to you and to be supported to change these behaviours, so that your overall health and well-being is not affected.

Understanding the different presentations of eating disorders can be difficult: the symptoms and behaviours do not always fit into the defined categories, and you do need to consider your own experience of these difficulties to get a true understanding of your own distress and pain. Different types of eating disorders can have symptoms in common. It may also be that your experience varies, and the type of symptoms can shift over time from one type of difficulty to another. It can be helpful to think about eating disorders as being on a spectrum or continuum. Some researchers have suggested that there are common factors that present across all the eating disorders. This work has been summarized in the development of the 'transdiagnostic model' developed by Fairburn and his team.[3] This model is very interesting in relation to understanding how symptoms and behaviours can change over time.

What causes eating disorders?

Eating disorders can affect every social and age group, and most commonly occur in adolescence, when there are many emotional, social and developmental challenges. There is so much more to eating disorders than a desire to alter one's body shape or weight. Various development crises and conflicts such as challenges with parents, insecurities in social development and the search for identity and autonomy can be reflected in the refusal or excessive intake of food. Your eating disorder may be a way of dealing with feelings that you are finding difficult to communicate, such as anger, worry, guilt or sadness, or numbing psychological distress caused by various life challenges. These challenges can be different for every person, and wide-ranging: there may be school or work challenges, friendship and relationship issues, or specific traumas such as bereavement or transitions. These feelings can develop in relation to life changes and transitions, leading you to feel out of control of your life. So an eating disorder might be a way of taking control over your life through your food intake and weight; sadly, the eating disorder can take on a controlling nature of its own. Eating disorders have also been linked to low self-esteem and self-confidence and personality characteristics such as perfectionism. This in turn leads to a complicated picture when trying to understand the development of an eating disorder; there is rarely just one issue that can be simply understood. It is thus more helpful to think of your eating disorder as having a wide range of causes rather than trying to focus on one specific issue, and to explore together with the people supporting you the meaning and the function that the eating disorder is having in your life.

How common are eating disorders?

There is a general idea that eating disorders seem to be increasing, and this is supported by the findings of the most recent research.[4]

We know that eating disorders can occur at any age, but studies also suggest that the age at which difficulties start tends to be lower than previously, impacting on how the illness will develop over the longer term and increasing the need for more treatments that are appropriate for young people. Adolescence can be a time of particular high risk. Adolescence is in fact generally a very busy time for development, with emotional, social and biological changes, so the impact of malnutrition on this process can have a negative effect on how young people recover from this difficult time.

Eating disorders have also long been associated with women; however, the number of young men diagnosed with eating disorders has also increased. Whilst binge eating behaviours and compensatory behaviours (e.g.

purging, fasting, excessive exercise) are not so common in young patients, there does seem to be a continuum between bulimia nervosa and anorexia nervosa, with young people moving between these two disorders over time.

The COVID-19 pandemic and the impact on eating disorders

The COVID-19 pandemic has created an unprecedented increase in the number of people suffering from eating disorders.[5] Recent research helps capture more specific information about the increase. Lin and colleagues found that over the pandemic inpatient care admissions and outpatient assessments had increased: more young people were presenting for treatment.[6]

It is very important to understand this in more detail. Lin and colleagues suggested that the COVID-19 pandemic presented the 'perfect storm' for eating disorders. The unusual set of circumstances created by measures trying to combat the pandemic combined to promote several risk factors for the development of eating disorders. The public health strategies developed to help contain the spread of the virus, such as stay-at-home restrictions, quarantine measures, self-isolation and social distancing, increased social isolation for many. The sudden change of life, such as the closures of school, universities and workplaces, meant an enforced shift to online communications. The consequence of this was that the security and routine that normally helped people to thrive in their lives was at best severely compromised, and at worst lost completely. At the same time, as a way of trying to manage the impact of these changes, there was a surge in internet use. This resulted in people being online or on the screen for large proportions of their day, which may have increased exposure to unhelpful and harmful social media messages and influences. It also meant that they were challenged with seeing their own image in the corner of the screen for large periods of time, whether it be related to schooling, social connectedness or even therapy or healthcare.[7] For those who worked in certain sectors of society there would have been additional anxiety and stress regarding meaningful employment and financial security – not to mention the health anxiety created by a new virus that, for many clinically vulnerable groups, was a serious threat to life.

Another consequence of public health restrictions put in place due to COVID-19 was the changes in the way that healthcare was delivered. At the start of the pandemic the message was to stay home to protect healthcare services from being overwhelmed and to reduce the transmission of the virus. All healthcare capacity was dedicated to support-ing the management of the pandemic and minimizing the strain on an overstretched healthcare system. As a result, many people did not seek support for fear of using vital ser-vices and for fear of contracting the virus. In short, people were too scared to ask for help and did not see their diffi-culties as a priority considering the nature of the healthcare crisis. Overall, whilst this meant that healthcare services were not overwhelmed in the way that was feared, it also meant that people did not seek the care they needed, or they were delayed in seeking this care. Furthermore, when care was sought, the changes in how it was delivered, such as a temporary pause on face-to-face assessment and longer-term delays in the provision of face-to-face interventions, meant that treatment interventions were experienced in a very different way.

In the sessions we had during the pandemic, we reflected together on how the pandemic was disrupting people's routines, and also the eating disorder's routine. Any type of eating disorder is in fact tightly bound to a set of structured rules around eating, compensatory behaviours and exercise. For example, Martha reported that she felt very overwhelmed by not being able to have time on her own at home, when she would normally binge. Gregory was the opposite: as he lived on his own, he suddenly felt segregated, and the sense of loneliness was so unbearable that only eating a large amount of food would alleviate it. Jim was used to going out to buy tiny portions of food several times a day and he did not have that opportunity any more. His family did not yet know about his difficulties with food, and he was forced to rely on his mother's shopping, which was extremely anxiety provoking.

We all had to adjust to online sessions, and initially many people worried about lack of privacy or missing the human contact and reassurance provided in the therapy room. With those who are still working with us, we can now look back and remember how important it was for us to be able to carry on our work together in such a difficult time. As therapists, more than ever we had to share our vulnerabilities and uncertainties, exactly like them, as we were also facing the pandemic for the first time. Now that things seem a bit more settled, talking about how people have experienced the pandemic, the strategies they adopted and the losses they faced is an important part of the initial assessment, but also of the therapeutic work. We would therefore like to encourage all of you to talk about your experience when you see a professional, as knowing and reflecting on how we cope with major stresses is very important to understand more about ourselves and the type of support we need.

At the time of writing, it is not clear whether the eating disorder increase currently being experienced will continue. As it stands, across the majority of the world restrictions have now been lifted completely. For the first time in almost two years there are no public health restrictions in relation to the COVID-19 pandemic. What, though, is not clear is what this means for mental health. Whilst many are very keen for life to return to a pre-pandemic normal, many are feeling lost and bewildered by the speed of the abandonment of restrictions and the seemingly sudden movement to living with COVID-19. Belkin and colleagues predict that the negative mental health effects of COVID-19 remain massive, far-reaching and long term.[8] We need to move away from feeling disempowered and restricted, and once again embrace the opportunities that a full and varied life can create. Some will achieve this, desperate for the freedom and liberty after two years of feeling deprived and restricted. Some will make tentative steps to change their lives back to something more tolerable and comfortable. Currently it is not clear what level of mental health support will be needed to pave the way towards a post-pandemic life, or what this will mean for the people struggling with eating disorders.

As a result of the increase in the prevalence of eating disorders, new guidelines have been published by the Royal College of Psychiatrists outlining the guidance for managing medical emergencies in the treatment of eating disorders.[9] This document replaces previous guidance, Junior MARSIPAN, which focused on the management of really sick patients under the age of 18 years with anorexia nervosa.[10]

The new guidance acknowledges that within all eating disorders there can be medical emergencies, rather than just focusing on anorexia nervosa. This is a very positive step forward in terms of healthcare systems acknowledging the physical and psychological risks of any form of eating disorder.

Overall, the pandemic confirmed that in a time of great distress, where the connection between the inside and outside world is disrupted, our food and our bodies can become like objects, through which we try to compensate for our unmet emotional, social and relational needs. For example, the fear of becoming unwell can lead one to overinvest in the idea of being healthy. Many adults and young people became very focused on exercise and healthy eating during the pandemic. For others, the sense of loneliness and isolation was addressed by overeating, and their relationship with food became a surrogate for real relationships.

Another important aspect is that the pandemic forced each one of us to face and deal with our vulnerability and fragility, from both a physical and an emotional point of view. It has reintroduced, in our overachieving and hyperactive Western society, the importance of acknowledging personal limitations. How to integrate and value this in our lives and our concept of our selves will be one of the challenges of the coming years.

Risk assessment and the importance of physical risk management

It is important that your weight is not the only consideration when assessing the immediate risk of your behaviours.

You may be a healthy weight but have physical symptoms such as lack of energy, mood swings, constipation, headaches, chest pain and lack of periods, to name just a few. Also, another very important aspect is the rate of weight loss. If you are losing weight very quickly this is particularly worrying. It is highly likely that you will be more physically unwell than those whose weight is stable but are considered underweight. So you do need to share this with those around you to get the support you need.

When evaluating risk, another factor to consider is calorie intake. However, your background history becomes very important here, in terms of how long and how much you have been restricting. At this stage you also need to consider if you are engaging in other unhelpful behaviours, such as overexercising, and if you are, then these behaviours put you at very high risk.

In terms of the physical risk associated with bulimia nervosa, purging behaviour occurring on a very frequent basis over a prolonged period of time can have serious physical consequences such as dizziness, severe fatigue and low mood. Blood sugars and levels of vitamins and minerals in your system can become depleted, creating other physical symptoms as well. It is very important that even if you do not feel ready to engage with specialized treatment, you see your medical doctor to check these parameters.

Finally, when assessing physical health, it is essential to assess emotional distress too: How are you feeling on a day-to-day, hour-to-hour basis? What type of support do you have around you? How isolated are you? Are the people around you able to help you?

In terms of risk assessment, it is important that all these aspects are considered, and we need to move away from the idea that only very severely underweight people need treatment.

Treatment approaches

When it comes to treatment approaches for eating disorders, various different therapies are available, which can make trying to get help quite confusing and complicated. The National Institute for Health and Care Excellence (NICE) is a UK-based regulatory body that evaluates all recent research trials and makes recommendations based on evidence of how effective the therapies are. The NICE guidelines are not only a reference for the UK, but also at an international level; they are valued by healthcare services across the world. You may have heard healthcare professionals refer to evidence-based therapies: these are ones that have been shown to be effective based on the evidence. The NICE guidance currently recommends that the main treatment approach for all eating disorders should be some form of psychological therapy.[11] Ideally this therapy should be provided in the community where possible. For some, particularly when their physical health is severely compromised by the symptoms of the eating disorder and progress is not being made with treatments being offered within the community, a more intensive type of treatment may be needed.[12] This could be in the form of a day hospital or partial hospitalization, where a person would attend a hospital treatment programme daily to access support with treatment. For others, a stay in hospital may be needed; this is referred to as inpatient care. This means that a person may be admitted to a specialist unit and could remain in hospital for a period of a few weeks or months to receive an integrated medical, nutritional and psychological treatment.[13]

The guidance also recommends that evidence-based therapies are offered by clinicians trained specifically in eating disorder treatments, and that therapies are tailored to the eating disorder rather than therapies that are non-specific. There should also be support in the form of nutritional advice and support to address other mental health needs or conditions that might co-exist. It suggests that a multi-disciplinary team is best placed to do this: this is a team that consists of a number of healthcare professionals from different fields, and ideally should involve a psychological therapist and a doctor. Additional support from dieticians, psychiatrists, occupational therapists and family therapists may also be helpful.[14]

Psychological therapies

There are several different types of psychological therapies available for the treatment of eating disorders. These can be different across the lifespan, with some therapies being more effective for children and adolescents, and others for adults.

Whilst there are several different forms of therapies, and different recommendations for children and young people and adults, all aspects of therapy provide something called psychoeducation. You may have heard this term before if you have been involved in healthcare services, as it is often talked about. Psychoeducation is a form of education provided by psychological therapists that offers people with mental health conditions information about their condition.

It contains information about the causes, symptoms, prognosis and treatments of their diagnosed condition. It can be a very important aspect of psychological treatment, as it will empower you to understand more about your condition, and this can impact positively on symptom management and prognosis and outcome. This feels particularly important in the treatment of eating disorders where the aspect of control and feeling disempowered by the illness are very evident. This can be the case whether you are an adult experiencing difficulty, a child or a young person, or if you are the support system around the person affected by the illness.

PSYCHOLOGICAL THERAPIES FOR ADULTS

For adults, psychological therapies that have been specifically adapted to treat symptoms of eating disorders have been found to have the strongest evidence base in terms of reducing symptoms. Enhanced cognitive behaviour therapy (CBT-E) is a very helpful treatment according to the NICE guidelines, and can be delivered in weekly sessions. The number of sessions needed is determined by the diagnosis. For example, anorexia nervosa has a longer treatment basis, with a recommended 40 sessions, whilst only 20 sessions are recommended for bulimia nervosa and binge eating disorder. Sometimes when symptoms are less severe, a brief type of CBT can be offered in the form of guided self-help, so in these instances you may be offered some support to work through a manual of treatment or self-help guide written especially with symptom management in mind. However, the evidence base for this type of treatment is not particularly strong, and following a treatment such as this, you may need more ongoing support in the form of further therapy.[15]

PSYCHOLOGICAL THERAPIES FOR YOUNG PEOPLE

If you are a young person with an eating disorder, focused family therapy for children and young people with anorexia nervosa or bulimia nervosa (FT-AN/FT-BN) is recommended by NICE.[16] This approach aims to support you and your family to recover and is a step-by-step treatment. The first step aims to build a good relationship between the therapist and you, your parents and other family members. Step two is to support you to establish a level of independence appropriate for your level of development with help from your family members. Finally, the third step focuses on plans for when your treatment ends and on managing any aspects of relapse.

Currently, this type of approach is most commonly offered in a community outpatient setting. For many it is helpful, but your family may struggle to engage effectively in this type of treatment for many different reasons. In these instances, NICE recommends two other forms of treatment: individual cognitive behaviour therapy that is focused on eating disorders (CBT-ED) or adolescent-focused psychotherapy for anorexia nervosa (AFP-ED). These approaches aim to reduce the risk to physical health and any other symptoms of the eating disorder.

As with adults, CBT-ED focuses on encouraging you to reach a healthy body weight through healthy eating. Therapy work involves psychoeducation and challenging the thoughts that are maintaining your eating disorder, work on understanding emotions, the negative perceptions of body image, improving self-esteem and self-confidence, and support to anticipate and manage moments of relapse. If you are a young person or adolescent, any work offered should be appropriate for the level at which you can work, whilst helping to enhance your self-belief and encourage the idea that things can be different.

AFP-ED is different from the CBT-ED, as it focuses more on emotions and relationships, and how these affect the eating disorder. The therapy aims to develop a shared understanding of your psychological issues and how your eating disorder behaviours are ways of helping you to cope in difficult moments. The aim of this is to support you as a person to develop alternative ways of coping that are better for managing distress and negative emotion. In later stages of treatment, issues relating to your identity and independence can also be explored.

If you are suffering with a binge eating disorder, or symptoms that relate to this, then the treatment that you may be offered could also involve the use of cognitive behavioural self-help materials. The aim of this is to promote engagement in a binge-eating-disorder focused guided self-help programme. If this approach is not helpful, group CBT-ED, focusing on psychoeducation and self-monitoring of the eating behaviour, can also be recommended. This approach will encourage you to think actively about your problems and help you identify goals to work on. This includes methods such as daily food plans, identifying potential triggers for binge behaviour, and body exposure training, which involves supporting you to identify and change negative beliefs about your body. This can be delivered as either a group or on an individual basis.

The use of medication

Medication is sometimes suggested for people with eating disorders. This can be in relation to the eating disorder symptoms, but it can also be recommended for other mental health conditions that co-exist with the eating disorder, such as anxiety and depression. If your experience has brought you into contact with healthcare services, you may have been offered some form of medication, and it is always important that you understand why, and what aspects of your difficulties the medication may support you with. There may be difficulties that you are struggling with in addition to the eating disorder. Sometimes symptoms of anxiety and depression can be made worse by the presence of eating disorder symptoms, and medication could be proposed to you by the medical team as an additional adjunct to your treatment. It is very important that this medication is carefully managed by a psychiatrist so that it can be integrated with other aspects of your treatment and care and to monitor its effectiveness. In contrast to psychological care, there are few medication options available for eating disorders. Of those, most have been used for the treatment of anorexia nervosa. Olanzapine, which belongs to the family of second-generation antipsychotics, has been found to have some benefits. In some instances, antidepressants from the family of selective serotonin reuptake inhibitors (SSRIs) have been found to have a positive impact on the co-existing mental health conditions.[17]

With regard to the other eating disorders, such as bulimia nervosa and binge eating disorder, there is some evidence that using a higher dose of SSRI has a slight impact on the management of symptoms. However, this ideally should not be offered as a stand-alone treatment but in conjunction with the use of psychological therapies.[18]

It is important that the medications are not seen as a quick fix to delegate the responsibility of the care. All medications can have several side effects, and it is important that the psychiatrist helps you to understand when and whether the benefits will outweigh the potential risks.

Towards more personalized treatments

Treatments for eating disorders are developing all the time. A recent large 22-year follow-up study of 228 women with anorexia nervosa or bulimia nervosa treated in a specialist centre found the majority (around two-thirds) recovered.[19] This is consistent with existing literature that tries to evaluate what works best for treatment and what is most effective.[20] Sadly, at this stage, we don't know enough about long-term outcomes for eating disorders, but we do know that treatment is very important, and that these difficulties rarely improve on their own.

Early intervention offers the best possibility for symptom change, and this is the best predictor of outcome across all eating disorders.[21] If you are suffering with any symptoms of an eating disorder, it is very important that you access support as soon as possible. Sometimes there are many delays in obtaining treatment, such as poor understanding, focus on weight management strategies rather than eating disorder support (particularly in the eating disorders where weight can remain stable or increase), stigma, shame and poor access to evidence-based therapies.[22]

When discussing different treatment approaches and the various clinical guidelines evaluating their effectiveness, it becomes evident that treatments are often evaluated in isolation, in relation to specific diagnostic criteria, rather than in combination. Clinical effectiveness is measured in a medical way defined by symptom reduction. In many respects this very rigid approach creates a paradox that is mirrored by the disorder. The disorder as we understand it is not solely about weight, body shape and food; it is about psychological distress, pain and suffering. However, as clinicians we can quickly begin to mirror the people in our care, with all our attention on weight and food rather than holding in mind the underlying pain and suffering that has created it. If this is your experience, it may lead to you feeling very frustrated, as the focus may be on nutrition and meal planning and you may want a different type of help.

However, there is more movement towards a broader understanding of symptoms and diagnostic criteria in the context of social and personal meaning. This encourages clinicians to understand mental suffering in its broadest context rather than just as disorders of the mind.[23] As experienced clinicians we are appreciating more and more the value and the effectiveness of a personalized approach that integrates the principles of many of the current interventions and the social and personal meaning that the disorder holds in the lives of you as our patients and also your families.

There are very few studies included in these evaluations that are co-produced, holding in mind these very important social and personal experiences. To move towards a position where the true meaning of the disorder is acknowledged, we need to understand more about the social and personal meaning of the eating disorder to inform the development of person-centred, experience-based approaches.

Given the importance of this approach, we would like to describe two studies that have considered feedback from people with eating disorders and their families. These studies describe feedback from patients and carers regarding treatment of anorexia nervosa for adolescents,[24] and specifically family-based therapy (FBT).[25] Both studies raise the issue of placing the responsibility for the patient learning to eat again and gaining weight on the parents. For those families who struggle to manage this task the sense of failure and guilt creates a paralysis that disempowers parents and carers. The feedback also raises concerns about the main emphasis being on eating, postponing a more meaningful understanding of the disorder until later stages of treatment. From a clinical perspective, there can be features of a person's presentations that may warrant an individualized plan that should inform treatment from the beginning rather than further down the pathway of recovery. This could depend on the severity of the illness, with some young people seeking treatment at an early stage, and others with a more severe form of the disorder.

Other important factors to consider in regard to more personalized treatments are co-morbid diagnoses (i.e. diagnoses of disorders that occur in addition to the eating disorder) related to neurodiversity. Disorders such as autistic spectrum disorder and attention deficit disorder are pervasive in nature, and will have an impact regardless of the severity of the eating disorder. The management difficulties that these diagnoses present regardless of the eating disorder need to be taken into account, and appropriate adaptations made to ensure treatments can be effective.

Tchanturia and their team explore much of this work in the development of the PEACE pathway (Pathway for Eating disorders and Autism developed from Clinical Experience), which aims to explore and understand the associations between anorexia nervosa and autistic spectrum disorders.[26] This pathway seeks to understand more about the prevalence of the co-existing conditions but also to evaluate and understand the necessary adaptations that need to be made to ensure that treatment is effective and accessible for this group, and to share this knowledge with others. This is just one example of a group of people with eating disorders who may need treatment to be adapted, and demonstrates why it is necessary to involve other people and families in the evaluation and development of further treatment approaches and pathways. Another group of people who may need a combination of treatments to help them with learning to eat again and gain weight are the people that fall into the severe and enduring group. Russell and colleagues propose that the clinical approach for this group should focus on the idea of rehabilitation rather than recovery, using a mixture of harm-reduction strategies, whilst still maintaining the hope that recovery is a possibility.[27]

In summary, treatment approaches that involve active feedback and evaluation from people with eating disorders, carers and clinicians are very useful and hold a potential for the future that is not yet realized. The potential to allow for broader thinking, more individualized formulations and interventions may lead to improved outcomes. It is just as important that they may also lead to a more meaningful experience of treatment, leaving people like yourself and your families with a better understanding of your disorder, and the care and support you receive.

Chapter 3

What Is So Important about Food?

Through this chapter we would like to invite you to think with us about the meaning associated with food and the relationship we develop with eating. We know that one of the main symptoms of an eating disorder is an unbalanced and dysregulated eating pattern. However, we do not ask ourselves enough why it is that food has become the target. Food is essential for all of us, and is also a means for us to mediate the relationships we have with other people and the social context. Even more, it is connected to our emotions and cultural traditions. The richness of possible meanings is so vast that we always dedicate a lot of time in therapy to exploring it. To help us reflect on the different meanings of food and our relationship with eating, we have used examples of conversations we have had in therapy to inform our writing.

Why does food become the enemy?

Whether you are a person with an eating disorder, a family member or a clinician, sooner or later you may pause and ask yourself, 'Why food? Why has food become the centre of attention and control, and a source of anxiety?' Strangely, this is not the first thing we ask ourselves as clinicians when we start learning about eating disorders. We take as a fact that the eating behaviours become altered, and we focus on how to help you to regulate them again. We get absorbed by their complexity and how the psychological and physical dimensions are interconnected.

People with eating disorders who come to us often describe their routine around eating and what are good and bad foods for them. Often, they say that they know that their eating patterns are different from before, and sometimes that causes distress and discomfort, but they are struggling to change them. Sometimes parents report to us that their young person never ate 'normally' but they did not feel that it was something that needed to be addressed. Others come to us saying that they had therapy for a few years but they may not have discussed these issues.

Many families who come to us are terrified that their child is eating less and less, and they find it very difficult to understand what is so challenging about eating. They should just eat, and they are telling them to eat, but with no success. When the problem is related to overeating instead of restriction, they describe it as being like a drug addiction or a lack of will power or discipline and control around food.

In the initial stage of treatment and therapy it is important to focus on overcoming the acute phase of the illness and to listen to how you describe food, and the emotions

50

related to it. Trying to interpret and explore the meaning associated with it might make you feel not heard and not understood at times. It is also very difficult at the beginning of the therapy process to talk about that which is most feared, and this can be very off-putting for many of you. We know there is a degree of shame associated with the fear of food, and exploring this can make you feel very vulnerable, so the safety of the therapy is very important if this is going to work. It can sometimes be the first big test of the therapeutic relationship.

After a while, though, when we feel we have created trust and connection with you, we can then pause and reflect with you on why food became the point of contention. There are some immediate and general meanings that we can attribute to food and eating, but it is important for you and your family to understand what food has represented for you specifically. After so many years of work in eating disorders, we still feel that we have not explored all the possible associations that could be made, but here we would like to share with you the main ones.

Food to survive

The first and most immediate meaning associated with food, which seems to be taken for granted, is that it is essential to survive. Food is fuel in this sense. If you don't eat, you die. If you eat too much, you experience discomfort and in the long term you cause damage to your body. Your body regulates the process of eating, so that when it needs food, you experience hunger, and when you have eaten sufficiently, you feel full. This process, which appears to be so simple, is completely altered when a person develops an eating disorder.

If food is essential to survival, then on some level when you have an eating disorder you can be questioning the core meaning of your own existence. Not necessarily because you feel you want to die, but because in that moment of your life you are debating your own identity, your purpose in life and your role in society. Food stops being a natural act, and it becomes something that requires to be thought about, and carefully thought about.

'Do I really have to eat? I want to choose and be in control. I don't want to depend on my body.'

'I don't need it really. I see other people eating so much and I am not like them. In the past I was, then I felt disgusted by myself. I won't go back there. And definitely, I won't eat what my family eats.'

'I don't deserve it. I have not worked enough. I will only eat healthy stuff. All my friends eat so little, I should be able to do the same.'

'If I eat, I will not be able to stop. It's happened many times – if something does not go as planned, then I feel I have broken the rules and I will eat everything I want in that moment. It's so good that I don't care if I will be bloated after. I will eat less tomorrow.'

From these words, what transpires is the need for these people with eating disorders to assert their independence from the conditions posed by the body. Sometimes you may feel judged and evaluated only on the basis of your body and what you eat, and rejecting the essential physiological need to eat is a way to take ownership of yourself again as a person with a purpose.

'I can do whatever I want with my body, so I want to be able to decide if and what to eat. I can control when and what to eat, without caring for the consequences.'

So you can see not only the act of independence from the body, but also from other people.

'I won't eat what my family eats, and I will eat less than my friends, because I am different from them. Or I want to be different – this is what can make me special and help me to occupy a place in the world.'

Through an eating disorder you may be asking yourself who you are, and what makes you different from others. You don't live only to survive, you want your life to have meaning, and make a difference. Questioning the act of eating and the power you can have over your body is a way to pose these crucial questions.

Food to be (or not to be) with others

Familial bonds

Another aspect which will be very clear to you all is that when you are born, you are totally dependent on your parents or other caregivers to feed you. This is also related to survival, as you would not be able to feed yourself if you were left alone. Therefore, you are not only dependent on food, but you are also, at least for a few years, dependent on another person to keep you alive by providing all sorts of nurturing, which includes food. You don't have any alternative but to trust that person. You are completely vulnerable and dependent on others to meet all your needs.

With the passing of time, however, as babies and young children, you will be able to start choosing, selecting and also rejecting food. There will be those of you who as children ate everything that was provided and made the process very simple. Others will have been picky and selective, or explorative and curious. You can observe some traits of your personality in these responses to food, but all these behaviours will also have something to do with the relationships you have with your caregivers. That original trust and bond through the relationship with food is questioned time and time again throughout life.

In fact, when an eating disorder breaks the serenity of family life, the relationship between you and the people around you almost capsizes: your parents may be unable to support you to eat in the way they have done in the past. They feel powerless in the face of the very first thing they did when you, as the child, came to life. It does not matter whether you as their child are eight, fifteen, twenty or forty years old; or if you as their child are starving, overeating or purging. In that moment the world stops, because eating is essential, and so when there are problems with it the people around you will often feel lost.

There are several kinds of behaviours related to eating with the family, from eating apparently normally with them and then emptying or purging food when alone or, conversely, bingeing in secret, to not even sitting at the table and rejecting any offer of food. Faced with these behaviours, families and partners will be asking themselves what went wrong, what has changed, why they can't help. Eating, therefore, is not only a biological need, but also a relational act that can connect or disconnect you from others.

Mila often talked about her decision to become vegan and eat less than the rest of her family, who she felt had always treated her as a child or as an extension of themselves, as a way to separate herself from them. She wanted to show them that she had her own ideas, and that she was more ethical and made more balanced food choices than them.

> 'My parents think that when I recover from anorexia I will go and feast with them again and eating all that cheese and meat. They have not realized yet that I am not that person any more. Or maybe I never was. I can eat more and protect myself; I can find that type of compromise, but I want to be my own person.'

Sometimes the attempt to differentiate and develop your identity can be a more hidden act. Everything may seem normal on the surface, but in secret and when alone, you binge and/or purge, which can provoke great physical and emotional suffering and trap you between the pressure to conform to expectations and liberating yourself through transgression and breaking the rules of normal and healthy eating.

Inevitably, it becomes essential to explore in therapy the eating habits of the family, through which we can gradually explore and identify relational patterns.

Social and peer influence

Often parents look for a specific cause of the eating disorder within the family. Although family values and relational dynamics always play an important part in the development of our identities, and therefore also on the development of symptoms, the world does not end within the walls of our home. The family itself is also influenced by the broader social and cultural context. The less you are aware of the impact of social values and tendencies, the more likely you are to be vulnerable to them, and you may express yourself through explicit choices and decisions. The social context provides ways in which people with eating disorders then manifest their suffering. In other words, the social context shapes the form and content of the symptoms.

The most immediate example in the field of eating disorders is the pressure of the ideal of thinness, and more broadly the importance attached to our external image, which needs to conform to certain aesthetic and societal standards. On the one hand, as someone who has an eating disorder or is developing an eating disorder, you may feel you have to conform to the expected image to be part of your peer group, but on the other hand you take it to extremes (becoming underweight or overweight) that are not sustainable, forcing yourself through the vicious cycle of suffering, to question whether you really believe in that ideal, or what its meaning and function are in your life.

Another example is related to healthy eating and veganism. With the development of different eating philosophies, we have observed the emerging of orthorexia. 'Orthorexia' is the term for when an interest in healthy eating and veganism becomes an obsession with eating only 'pure' foods, and is seen as an early indicator in some people who develop an eating disorder. The focus on being healthy taken to an extreme leads to the person seeing themselves as an efficient and productive machine that can closely monitor itself. Amy once said in a session that she noticed how much tracking and monitoring there was in her life. She wore a watch that monitored her sleeping, breathing and activity patterns. She knew how many calories she was eating and how many steps she was taking every day, and she discussed these with her peer group.

Being on a diet and talking about different types of diets has become popular and can be difficult to avoid, to the point that people often tell us that they think we are all suffering from an eating disorder to some degree. Food is so central in our lives nowadays that people are keen to tell others what they eat – whether they are omnivorous, pescatarian, vegetarian or vegan. Nonetheless, what does decrease for people with an eating disorder is the experience of conviviality, and the enjoyment of all the social aspects of eating together. In fact, one of the first warning signs of the development of an eating disorder is social disconnection and withdrawal. It is only later that the person's eating habits will also alter.

Food to feel

Every family, depending on their cultural traditions and customs, share preferences for specific foods and ways to prepare them, which over time will gain a strong emotional connotation. You may tend to link specific foods and dishes to memories of specific events, places and people and the emotions you felt then. You should all be able to recall some childhood memories related to food eliciting positive or negative emotions. Perhaps certain dishes prepared for special family or social occasions are still very impressed on your mind. Thinking about those dishes may take you back to the warmth of the relationships you had with the people involved, their care in preparing meals, and the joyful atmosphere at these events.

Emotions can also impact on your appetite and the way you eat. When anxious, you may tend to eat less, or you may feel full of emotion and be unable to eat. Or those emotions may trigger the urge to binge or overeat as a way of escaping the difficult emotion you are experiencing. Anger can lead us to eat quickly, devouring not only the food but also, symbolically, the person you had an argument with a few moments earlier. But perhaps if that person is still in front of you, you may refuse to sit and eat with them as a way of expressing your rejection. And we have probably all have heard someone say, 'Don't talk to me now as I haven't had the chance to eat yet and I am so irritable.' The examples are countless.

Some people may think that the act of eating is a simple, rational act of will and that it should therefore be sufficient to convince you that you should eat, and you will then be able to do it. Or that they could explain all the negative consequences of binging and purging and you will then just stop. But as we know, it is not that simple. In that moment, you are unable to identify and understand your emotions, and the eating behaviour is replacing the expression of your emotions in a way that is explicit and visible. It becomes important that we ask ourselves, and that you ask yourself, how we can explore the emotions behind your eating and what message you are trying to communicate.

Furthermore, the sense of will power and discipline is already at the core of the eating disorders and does not have to be reinforced with the message 'If you want, you can do it.' On the contrary, it is important to help you to take into account your subjective preferences and needs. Food has so many functions in your life, and it can play many roles when it becomes the point of contention in eating disorders. It can be merely fuel to just survive, an object to control, an enemy to challenge and dominate, a friend always there to comfort you, a flag to wave in the sky to announce your new identity. It can represent all these things, but it is none of them. As Francesca said after a few years of therapy:

> 'As my therapist you listened to me for hours and hours talking about food and dissecting it and hating it. I feel better now, I know myself more. And I have realized that, after all, it wasn't about food, was it?'

Francesca, you are right. It wasn't about food at all.

Chapter 4

Why Don't I Like My Body?

Like food, your body is at the centre of the dispute in eating disorders. Why is your body under attack? The experience of your body is one of the most complex and therefore delicate experiences. The journey starts as soon as you are born, if not even before, through the connection you have with your mother in the womb. It is ever changing and never defined once and for all. When you think about your body you may deal with some duplicity. We can say that you have a body, but also that the body represents you. You may think that your body is your own and only your own, but it is co-constructed through the relationship you have with others, and also influenced by the way other people see it and your experience of their evaluations of your body and comments they might make. Therefore, the development of your body self-awareness and body image is an ongoing interactive process.

The body has biological and physiological limitations, but within your mind you would like it to reach certain ideal standards close to perfection. Sadly, when you suffer, your body is deprived of its vitality, because when you measure it according to ideal standards, and look at each part of it with criticism, it is being treated like an object. Sometimes you may deny it the right to exist in its needs and spontaneity. However, what you are really aiming for, throughout all your life, is to finally feel at home and content in your own body. This is something that may feel quite distant from where you are right now.

I have a body, I am my own body

It is through your body that you present yourself to the world, and the image you have of your body in your mind comes from the experiences you have in, and with, the external world. Your body not only belongs to you, but it is you, so much so that you can say not only 'I have a body', but also 'I am my body': a subject who feels, thinks, perceives and acts, and who therefore has a relationship with the world. 'As soon as you wake up, the experience begins: I am...the body...in the world. It may seem that it develops in sequence, but in reality, it happens simultaneously: it is a single idea of having a body in the world.' This is the holistic view of human beings expressed by a humble peasant from India, Sri Nisargadatta Maharaj, who in a certain period of his life managed to reach the 'realization of his own Self'.[1] He says that having and being our own body in the world is a single idea that we experience all at once.

This duplicity of 'I have a body' and 'I am my body' makes the experience of your body one of the most delicate and fragile experiences, and it is therefore central to psychological research,[2] and to the understanding of the reasons why your body is under attack in eating disorders. It is difficult to keep in mind this duplicity, because when you think about your identity, you often tend to separate the mind from your body.

Today we know that what happens in our minds is very connected with biological, brain and genetic factors, and what, for convenience and tradition, we define as 'mind' cannot be artificially separated from what we mean by 'body'. Nonetheless, in order to distinguish ourselves from other people, and to define our identity, we have to see and experience our own body. In doing so, we want our body to be seen, acknowledged and respected; we want to build a home for our body.

However, when we struggle or when we suffer, then the experience of having and being a body becomes confused and fragmented. Our body becomes a surface where we draw our individuality, express our obsessions or discomfort, or write our pain in a visible and sometimes indelible way. This is why any kind of bodily practices, from tattoos and piercing to extreme diets, surgeries and self-harm, can be considered as forms of support for our identities. The bodies of people full of fears, in search of their own place in the world, become the theatres of conflicts and representations of different parts of our identity. The body ceases to be a natural reality to be lived and experienced, and becomes instead an object to analyse, to inspect, to control, to harm. The body is not perceived, but thought of, in a repetitive and obsessive way, by claiming the right to freely dispose of it, to free it from all material conditions such as hunger, fullness, pain, tiredness, with the aim to access an ideal dimension of total suspension from living.

The development of body image

The body plays a central part in the definition of your identity and experience of relationships with others. Your body self-awareness is influenced by thought, and emotional and social processes, which all give a sense of continuity to your body experience.

The mental representation of your body begins very early. The basis of the development of body image and your satisfaction or dissatisfaction with your physical appearance is in fact influenced by the relationships you have with your caregivers and later with your peer group, your first emotional and sexual experiences, and the external socio-cultural values and standards of the place you live.

The sense of self, which begins at the moment of birth, develops in the first years of life, when the child slowly develops a sense of the boundaries of the body: the external boundary of the body becomes more and more specific and delimited. Reciprocal interactions with parents shapes both the internal and external sensations of the body, creating the child's body image. The boundaries of the body create a sort of membrane between what is 'me' and what is 'not me', and the child learns to identify the limits of their own body, that is, where their body ends and where the external environment begins.

The first sense of self is experienced through tactile, visual and auditory stimuli, which help the child distinguish their own body from the external environment. In particular, the parents' hands define the boundary of the child's body, and the child's face is delimited by their parents' soft and warm caress.

The way parents come into physical contact with the

64

child and play with them has an important role in the development of the body image: the newborn knows nothing about their body and must be able to distinguish it from other objects in the environment through physical sensations. Adequate body sensory stimulations, such as massages, rocking and contacts of various kinds with the parent's body, are important for the development of the child's body image at an early age.

At around three months of age, babies begin to distinguish themselves from others. Up to four to five months, they are attracted to the image of their mother reflected in the mirror, but not to their own, and at nine months they start perceiving the sense of their own continuity. In the following months they begin to be aware of the existence of a relationship between themselves and other images, until they develop, between 12 and 18 months, the ability to recognize themselves.

From the age of 12–18 months, coinciding with self-recognition, the child develops self-awareness and self-perception with distinct physical and emotional qualities. The moment in which the child recognizes their own image in the mirror is considered a reliable and decisive sign that they have achieved a sense of their own identity. Self-recognition in the mirror requires complex mental and symbolic skills, similar to those needed to produce words.

Over time, the child sees themselves as separate and different from their caregiver, and consolidates a stable representation of themselves. The body becomes the pivot of their growth, and it is felt more and more to be distinct from others. At the age of six, their body image becomes clearer.

The first kinds of self-awareness, which emerge around

two years of age, are related to the process of separation from the caregiver and are expressed through the ability to recognize bodily perceptions such as hunger or tiredness, and to communicate them through signals such as crying or laughter. In this phase, the child can use food to communicate with the adult: the acceptance or rejection of food is related to autonomy, and the exploration of distance from or closeness to the caregiver. The child's feeling of body identity strengthens between the age of three and five with the discovery of having a male or female body.

During the primary school period, due particularly to the continuous and inevitable confrontation with other children, another important element of the body image appears, which is that linked to the physical and psychological sense of their competence and ability.

Starting from pre-adolescence, the certainties relating to our own body disappear. We are urged to build new ones, on the basis of physical changes, and social expectations with regard to body identity. In most cases, a child's body is in good health and is predictable, whilst during adolescence the body begins to feel unsettled and start to rumble. The physical transformation linked to puberty and the impetuous, sometimes unexpected, onset of sexual maturity challenge the image of the body gradually built by the child. After long years of calm, the hormonal systems, present since birth, are activated, and trigger the modification of the child's self-image.

Many aspects of the individual personality, such as self-esteem and self-confidence, can also influence the development of body image in adolescence. Another important building block of personality is perfectionism, which can push the adolescent to invest their resources towards unrealistic physical ideals, sometimes at all costs, in order to gain others' approval.

When the body appears distant from the desired one, the emotional discomfort can manifest as disordered eating behaviours and alteration of sleep and hygiene patterns. In adolescence, one is in the world through the body, and that is why the body may start to suffer. When the crisis occurs, it seems difficult to live with the body as it is in the present, but at the same time, it is difficult to accept a body different from the previous one. A tendency to inspect the body in the mirror repeatedly and with anguish, and obsessive attention to physical appearance, in the hope that perceived flaws may disappear, are the most accurate expressions of the collapse of the personal identity. Not only is the body experienced in its changes, but it is also no longer 'my' body, and, in the loss of the limits that separate it from the social world, it becomes the body of others. Our ideas about our own bodies depend not only on the experience of the body, but also on comparison with others and their opinions. This process of reciprocal relationships, which begins in the first years of life, is long-lasting and, although it reaches relative stability in some phases of life, it never ends.

The inability to see ourselves

The literature dedicated to body image is very rich. Many authors from very different disciplines, such as philosophers, psychologists, psychiatrists and physicists, have carried out a lot of research throughout the past century.

According to the philosophical reflections of Merleau-Ponty, the body cannot be objectified, because, unlike anything else in the world, it is constantly perceived and experienced.[3] None of us can have a faithful image of our body. What we think about our body is the result of a construction process rather than a discovery. The image we have of our own self is something that the body creates. If we think about our body in terms of physical appearance, the main condition we have to accept is that it is difficult to look at and see ourselves completely. We can lower our head and see our feet, legs, stomach, hands, arms, shoulders and chest, only from a very close perspective, and that's about it. We can't see anything else. We can look at ourselves in the mirror, but that is only a reflection of our image. The same goes for photographs or videos. These are reflections of our appearance, and we need tools like mirrors and cameras to obtain them. The body image is a concept that we create in our mind, through our several perceptions and the assessments that we make regarding our physical appearance, and consists of many dimensions. Wishing to obtain a well-defined body image, we will always try to gain new information, and for its construction and organization we use not only present experiences, but also past ones, through our memory, which has the function of preparing the material for a new construction and organization.

If our identity is not determined once and for all, the value and meaning of the body image is always changing and temporary, since we are subjected to our own but also other people's gaze. This is why the experience of our body is developed through an interactive process. Other people describe us and make comments about how we look, so we can see ourselves through their eyes. Each person will provide a description that will always have to be considered subjective, influenced by the relationship they have with us, and their personal beauty standards. Furthermore, that description will have a certain value based on what the social and cultural contest will judge as good, pleasant and attractive.

We need others in order to have a more comprehensive sense of how we look. How does it feel to think about this, that our own view can only be a partial view to be integrated with that of others? Does it give you a sense of instability, uncertainty, over-reliance on the views of others?

Often, the way we see ourselves is not the same as others see us. We can see some details that other people do not notice that much, or vice versa. Who are we then? How do we look? Are we the person we think we know and see, or the person described by others?

Let's consider Laura's experience, for example. She knew that her nose was a bit crooked, but it had never been an issue, until her boyfriend pointed it out and described it as a very big defect that was ruining the rest of her beautiful face. He went so far as to encourage her to 'correct' it through plastic surgery. Many arguments followed, which impacted on not only her self-confidence, but also on the stability of their relationship.

Laura's experience is somewhat well represented by a famous novel by the Italian writer Pirandello, *One, No One, and One Hundred Thousand*,[4] where the protagonist, Vitangelo Moscarda, discovers by way of a completely irrelevant question that his wife poses to him that everyone he knows, everyone he has ever met, has developed Vitangelo's *persona* in their own imagination and that none of these personas corresponds to the image of Vitangelo that he himself has developed and believes himself to be. The novel begins with discussion of his nose. It is interesting to read this conversation, as it is similar to the many conversations we often have with our partners and friends about big or small details of our body.

'What are you doing?' my wife asked me, as she saw me lingering, contrary to my wont, in front of the mirror.

'Nothing,' I told her. 'I am just having a look here, in my nose, in this nostril. It hurts me a little, when I take hold of it.'

My wife smiled.

'I thought,' she said, 'that you were looking to see which side it is hangs down the lower.'

I whirled like a dog whose tail has been stepped on:

'Which side hangs down the lower? My nose? Mine?'

'Why, yes, dear,' and my wife was serene, 'take a good look; the right side is a little lower than the other.'

I was twenty-eight years old; and up to now, I had always looked upon my nose as being, if not altogether handsome, at least a very respectable sort of nose, as might have been said of all the other parts of my person. So far as that was concerned, I had been ready to admit and maintain a point that is customarily admitted and maintained by all those who have not had the misfortune to bring a deformed body into the world, namely, that it is silly to indulge in any vanity over one's personal lineaments.

And yet, the unforeseen, unexpected discovery of this particular defect angered me like an undeserved punishment. It may be that my wife saw through this anger of mine; for she quickly added that, if I was under the firm and comforting impression of being wholly without blemishes, it was one of which I might rid myself; since, just as my nose sagged to the right—

'Something else?'

Yes, there was something else! Something else! My eyebrows were like a pair of circumflex accents, ^^; my ears were badly put on, one of them standing out more than the other; and there were further shortcomings—

'What, more?' Ah, yes, more: my hands, the little finger; and my legs (no! surely, they were not crooked!)—the right one was bowed slightly more than the other, toward the knee—ever so slightly.

Following an attentive examination, I had to admit that all these defects existed. It was only then, when the feeling of astonishment that succeeded my anger, had definitely changed to one of grief and humiliation—it was only then that my wife strove to console me, urging me not to take it so to heart, since with all my faults, when all was said, I was still a handsome fellow. I made the best of it, accepting as a generous concession what had been denied me as a right. I let out a most venomous 'thanks,' and, safe in the assurance that I had no cause for either grief or humiliation, proceeded to attribute not the slightest importance to these trifling defects; but I did confer a very great and extraordinary importance upon the fact that I had gone on living all these years without ever once having changed noses, keeping the same one all the time, and with the same eyebrows and the same ears, the same hands and the same legs—and to think that I had had to take a wife, to realize that they were not all that they should be.

'Huh! small wonder in that! Doesn't everybody know what wives are for? Made, precisely, for discovering a husband's faults.'

True enough, mind you—I don't deny this about wives. But I may tell you that, in those days, I was prone to fall, at any word said to me, at the sight of a housefly buzzing about, into deeps of reflection and pondering that left me with a hollow feeling inside, and which rent my soul from top to bottom and tore it inside out like a molehill, without any of all this being visible on the outside...

Coming back now to the discovery of those slight defects, I was immersed all of a sudden in the reflection that it meant—could it be possible?—that I did not so much as know my own body, the things which were most intimately a part of me: nose, ears, hands, legs. And turning to look at myself once more, I examined them again. It was from there that my sickness started, that sickness which would speedily have rendered me so wretched and despairing of body and of mind that I should certainly have died of it or gone mad, had I not found in my malady itself the remedy (I may say) which was to cure me of it.[5]

From that conversation, Vitangelo realized that the representation he had of himself was different from the representation that others had, and each of them could have a different representation of him, making him feel like a stranger to himself. The perception of some details of his body led him to reflect on the construction of his identity. In the same way, Laura had to start questioning why she felt so vulnerable at the criticism from her boyfriend, and how that comment had little to do with her body, but was very much related to her self-esteem and the quality of the relationship she was in.

The obsession to see ourselves

Knowing that we cannot completely see ourselves, and feeling at the mercy of others' descriptions, comments and judgements, leads us to look for ways to increase the certainty of what we see and to perfect what we think others might see. Society has been overwhelmed by the era of the selfie and the thousands of filters that can be used to 'correct and perfect' our images in the pictures. Many parents tell us that their children spend countless hours locked in their rooms in front of the mirror or look at themselves over and over again in every shop window. Questions about how we look and if others like us can be endless, and never really meet our need for certainty and reassurance.

When we are so worried about our looks, what are we really worried about? We, the authors, think it is about the need to feel accepted by the others. It is related to the need to feel safe in relationships and fulfil a sense of social belonging. To feel that we belong, we know that it is important to meet the standards required by that specific context, but at the same time we don't want to be just a copy of other people, so we also want to differ by being better than others at representing a certain style. On the contrary, if we don't want to belong to a certain group, then we will build our own unique style to convey our individualities.

Body image consists of many components: perceptual (how we visualize the size and shape of our own body); attitudinal (what we think and know about our body); affective (what feelings we have towards our body); and behavioural (nutrition and physical activity). If we consider all these components, we can understand how a person's body image relates to the person as a whole, in all aspects of their being.

In eating disorders, worries about physical appearance become obsessions, which do not have anything to do with vanity, but more with the role that the person would like to play within a group and the broader social context, and the representations of their identity. There is no search for an ideal of beauty and youth per se. Rather, people with eating disorders pursue the desperate attempt to recognize their own identity through their body, which becomes like an object, an empty envelope to be modified, injured and hated in order to feel alive. The process of objectification causes deep suffering that leads the person to question themselves again and again about their own subjective and personal value.

George was only 17 when he started thinking a lot about his future and the person he wanted to be. He had a strong sense of responsibility, morality and empathy. He wanted to help others and make a difference. He seemed to strive for the classical Greek ideal of *kalos kagathos*, of a complete human personality, harmonious in mind and body, beautiful and virtuous. He spent hours in front of the mirror, worrying about little asymmetries between the right and left side of his body. Unsure about his sense of self and identity, he was looking for symmetry in his body to give him a steady direction in his life.

'You won't hurt me any more!'

In any relationship, we are exposed to the risk of being hurt, physically and emotionally. The closer we are to someone, the greater the risk. When we love another person, we want to develop a connection and trust with them. This makes us feel dependent on them. We feel the need to spend time with them, and to tell them about ourselves. We would like to have a place in their mind and heart and to know that they depend on us too. All of this, which belongs to the beauty of attachment and love, is also what makes us vulnerable and fragile, at the mercy of others.

The first relationship of love and empathy that involves nurturing and intimacy is the one between a parent and a child. It is based on full reciprocity and is essential for the satisfaction of our vital needs. It is so necessary for our survival that any disruption in it can cause a sense of anguish and loss. All the other relationships that we form throughout our life are expected to be based on the same reciprocity, trust and intimacy that we should have experienced in our primary relationships.

Sometimes we are scared of experiencing need, dependence and love for another, because in any relationship of dependence and interdependence, it is impossible not to suffer at least a little. We are not certain that the other person will be able to understand, value and protect us. Or maybe they do not reciprocate our feelings and we feel dismissed, abandoned, even worthless at times. Whenever we feel hurt and disappointed by the other, we experience great suffering, and we feel the need to protect ourselves. We use specific ways to regulate our distance from the other to protect ourselves, such as crying, expressing anger, or isolating. A baby's cry has many purposes, one of which is to control the anger or the loss of the adult, by inducing alarm, pain and guilt in them and getting them to come close again.

Another way to protect ourselves against the suffering of love is emotional isolation. If a child goes through long phases of frustrated anger, they find that they can extinguish the pain by isolating themselves in their own internal world. In a similar vein, an adult can develop a sense of self-control and self-sufficiency in which they show themselves that they don't need anyone. In doing this they will also feel a sense of invulnerability. Sometimes, the suffering can be so strong that we want to build a wall between us and the other. 'You won't hurt me any more!' we say. 'I would rather be alone than allow you to make me feel so vulnerable.'

Luc told me that he would never allow himself to get close to someone again, so intense was the pain he experienced when his girlfriend broke up with him. Luc was 15 years old, and still uncertain what he was really feeling for Mary. But for the first time he felt he could rely on someone and be intensely connected. Was this a friendship, or romantic love? He did not know, and it didn't matter. Mary suddenly left him with no explanation, and only then Luc realized that Mary was not reciprocating his feelings. So Luc denied his love, rejecting it in order to defend himself.

> *'I would rather suppress all my needs, being alone, not getting close or attached to anyone, instead of finding myself doing self-harm and exhausting myself with endless hours of workout.'*

After the breakup, Luc started self-harming, by cutting himself in hidden parts of his body. All his emotional suffering was turning into physical pain. Cutting himself was like a ritual, a surgical procedure that made him feel in charge of himself. No one can inflict pain on me, if not myself.

These are very unhelpful thoughts that can reinforce risk behaviours and need further exploration and management. The reason some people get stuck in this cycle is that the physical pain can be defined and located in a specific part of the body. You can see the wound. It has a beginning and an end. It is there in front of your eyes, and you are the one inflicting it on yourself. It gives an apparent sense of control, and also a way to serve your sentence. The crime committed was giving your love and trust to another. You are the king and your own subject at the same time. It is painful, also very risky, but it seems emotionally safe. The body ceases to be your ally, a part of yourself, and it becomes just an object you can use at your own will. It is like a canvas on which to engrave your pain. However, the sense of control and safety is mistaken, as from a physical point of view these practices are very dangerous, and the emotional suffering will only become more and more intense because it cannot be processed through these behaviours.

Luc alternated self-harm with physical exercise in the form of running. He interpreted any sign of tiredness as a symptom of his many weaknesses, so he pushed himself harder and harder, because what he wanted was to feel strong, and superior to any form of suffering.

Initially, Luc had experienced a deep sadness, which could have led him to ask for emotional support from someone else, to seek comfort or to express his anger. However, the disappointment in how he felt mistreated by Mary led him to withdraw trust from others and to reject any other relationship. The self-harm rituals, reinforced by a false sense of self-control, led Luc to exclude himself from a social and sentimental life, and to numb himself.

Such control over the body takes the place of emotions, thoughts and reflections. The suffering Luc experienced could not be processed but got trapped in that repetitive pain of the self-harm procedures. He felt safer and not exposed to the mercy of Mary, or anyone else, but he was living in a cold and dark tunnel. The physical self-harm was accompanied by an extreme and solitary self-reliance, used as a form of safeguarding.

I told Luc that these self-harm behaviours were not allowing him to connect, process and overcome the difficult emotions he felt, leading him to relive over and over again the same traumatic experience. A self-inflicted physical pain is repetitive and can be never-ending. Connecting to the emotional suffering would be scary, like navigating in the open sea in the middle of a storm, but it would be transformative and would take him to the shore. He gradually developed some trust in me and stopped self-harming. He continued doing his workouts, but respected the messages sent by his body, and he realized that by doing that, he could better achieve his goals.

Anorectic eating behaviours are also a form of self-harm, with the same self-protective function. The control of appetite and weight represent the effort of the person to expel and deny the physiological need for food, which they interpret as weakness. As discussed above, the physiological need for food represents the psychological need for a convivial human relationship. In anorectic behaviours we see not only the control of food, but also of emotions, affections and relationships. In binge eating and purging behaviours, food and its expulsion is used in a way that always causes a numbness within the body and soul.

Self-harm behaviours have taken the form of a trendy phenomenon. Inflicting pain on our own body and putting ourselves at risk has now become a sort of global perversion that is streamed on the web. Self-harm is thus no longer considered to be a psychopathology, but as a complex form of moral transgression, which cannot be simply treated in the therapy room but also needs to be addressed from a psychosocial, political and cultural point of view.[6]

In today's society we have become experts in the medical management of people, and we consider our bodies as sacred objects to improve, perfect and medicalize. We have lost, though, the sense of vitality, conviviality and playfulness that can be expressed through our bodies. When she found out that she was pregnant, Julia put it this way: 'Time has found its own home in my body,' meaning that she did not impose on herself the age at which a woman is supposed to have children, as dictated by others, but she waited for and respected her own and her partner's timing.

We suffer greatly when we feel we don't have the right to impose our own timing and needs, or simply to truly communicate with the person we are in a relationship with. We are immersed in the wellness and medical industry that tells us how we should treat and perfect our bodies and that idealizes how we look on the outside. In a time of conflict and suffering, we use the same language offered by society, and we show that pain through our body. Any kind of self-harm practices put the conflict on stage. This can take the form of cutting, starvation, vomiting or overeating.

Luc was very frustrated that it was only when he started

self-harming that everyone (school, family and friends) got alarmed and sought support for him. He could not express his sadness in any other way, and no one had noticed that he was suffering. Many young people tell us something similar:

> 'You are all worried about me losing weight, but when I told you that I was struggling you said I was not sick enough, or I had to focus on my exams!'

Dangerous behaviours and the physical representation of suffering are dramatic attempts to claim back ownership of our bodies, linked to our feelings of self-worth. Luc felt that he did not have the right to suffer from the separation from his girlfriend Mary. He thought that he had to accept the fact that relationships and friendships are liquid and transient and to suffer in silence.

It is important that people are supported to voice buried feelings, and to value their individual identities and feelings, so that their battles against themselves can end and they are open to support from others. This cannot be done only in the therapy room but needs to happen in all social contexts.

Chapter 5

Is Recovery Possible?

When you develop an illness, you often feel paralysed; your life is seemingly on pause. The illness does not involve only you as the person affected, but also your family and the support system around you. An illness can completely change how you see yourself and your life in the present and in the future. It can create, within your life, conditions of great uncertainty, and at this point it may lead you to look for support and treatment. It is at this stage, before starting any form of treatment, that you and your family start asking yourself if recovery is possible, what recovery could look like, and what it means for each of you involved in the process. In this chapter we invite you to explore the questions you have about recovery, your perspective on recovery, and how it is similar to or different from the perspective of the people close to you. We briefly describe the main stories that develop around an illness and how they shape our view of the recovery process. We also consider the perspectives of the other people affected by the eating disorder, such as your family members, partners and friends.

The meaning of recovery

Questions

Questions about recovery are endless; when you find your-self stuck in a situation causing a lot of pain, naturally you want to know if there is going to be a solution, if you can truly recover your life: *'Can I ever be free from the eating disorder? Will my child be able to develop and flourish and enjoy a content and happy life? Or is the threat of the return of the illness at difficult periods of time something that will be with us forever? Will it cast a shadow over our lives, will it prohibit choices for fear of a return to the tyranny that the illness has created for them and for us as a family? How long does recovery typically take? What does it involve?'*

The first step in the recovery process is to open up the conversation about the meaning of recovery. When we start this conversation, it is very common for you and your family to ask us about our own experiences of recovery and what our thoughts are about this. This is a very logical pathway to follow: you are simply asking the perceived expert what their experiences are, and it is very understandable that you would want to hear this. At this stage, when working with a team of doctors, dieticians and so on, the therapist can often become the expert in the room; following on from this we become the member of the team who is perceived to hold the key to recovery.

However, because of the idiosyncratic and complex nature of the illness, it is very difficult to answer questions such as those mentioned above. There is also an awareness that the answers to these questions hold great value, and as the therapist you are placed in a position of responsibility, but the future outcome is impossible to predict. At times like these, the therapist is the holder of the hope that things can be different and that they have experience of this. It is important that therapists are able to hold this responsibility and manage the dynamics that it can create within the therapy setting. It feels very important that we are able to explore these questions, not only for you and your family, but for everyone who invests in reading our thoughts, and for those who trust us in the therapy room.

We know that it is possible to recover from an eating disorder, although it is difficult to find up-to-date and clear figures from research studies.[1] Perhaps more importantly, as therapists we *believe* that it is possible to fully recover from an eating disorder. If we did not truly believe this regardless of the research data, if we did not experience this on a regular basis through our work with people and families, it would feel very difficult to continue to do the work we do.

Considering all of the evidence and our experience of recovery, it is important to acknowledge that it is not an easy journey. It is a process that requires patience, honesty, self-forgiveness and hard work to see it through, from your perspective and also from the people around you such as your family and your friends.

Narratives

To help you explore what recovery could look like for you, we can summarize three common narratives about the course and resolution of an illness. Commonly, the plot line playing in our mind goes something like this: 'Yesterday I was healthy, today I'm sick, tomorrow I'll be healthy again.' This is a 'restitution' narrative. But there are also two other broad narrative types that ground ways to think about recovering from illness. The 'chaos' narrative imagines life never getting better again. In this case, the meaning of life has lost its internal coherence, and the illness is experienced as a fracture impossible to mend. Alternatively, an illness can be seen as a journey that becomes a 'quest', with the ill person holding a belief that something is to be gained from the experience.

In our Western culture, we are usually presented with 'restitution' narratives and their promise of health restoration in contrast to 'chaos' stories, which make for uneasy listening.[2] It is helpful to think this point through and try to understand whether your personal narrative is influenced by a narrative proposed by social media and cultural beliefs, because these narratives will shape your motivation towards treatment and the way you are going to engage with it. For example, someone living to a 'restitution' narrative would likely pursue, be hopeful of and expect recovery, whilst seeing the illness as a 'quest' would motivate the individual and their carers to explore the meaning behind the symptoms, and the function of the illness in their life.

Sometimes your narrative (the role and meaning you give the illness) can change throughout the course of the illness and be different between one member of your family and another. For example, initially you might feel pushed by others to change and get better, whilst for you there is no need to change. Even the idea of being healthy could be seen as something detrimental, that should not be pursued. This may be the case for many of you. If you are affected by anorexia nervosa, at the beginning of the illness regaining your health could mean going back to the time when you felt empty and ordinary. The parents of the person with the eating disorder tend to have a completely different view. At first, they see it as unsolvable chaos. They cannot see a way out because they do not even understand why you would want to stop eating or use food in such a destructive way in the first place. Later, they may shift from the 'chaos' to the 'restitution' narrative: if previously you were eating and were fine, recovery will help you to fix this; you will eat again, and everything will be fine as before.

As clinicians, too, we should be aware of our own narrative and how it is influenced by both our personal values and our clinical background. In our work, we tend to adopt a 'quest' narrative. For us, a psychological symptom is an attempt to find a new way of being in the world; they are an indication of unmet needs. The symptoms are encouraging people to review their values and the way they live, to think about their relationships and identity development.

In this sense we do not consider recovery simply as a reduction of symptoms. It is rather a journey of personal discovery, growth and the emergence of a new self. It is a deeply personal, unique process of changing personal attitudes, values, feelings, goals, skills and roles. It is a way of living a satisfying and hopeful life. Recovery involves the development of new meaning and purpose in your life as you grow beyond the catastrophic effects of mental illness. It is neither synonymous with cure nor does it simply involve a return to a previous state.[3] Rather, it is a lifelong process that involves an indefinite number of steps in various life domains. As a result, many people view the process of recovery as something that almost defies definition. It is often described as more an attitude, a way of life, a feeling, a vision or an experience, rather than a return to health or any kind of clinical outcome per se. In addition to being unable to return to your life prior to your illness, in recovery you may not want to go back to your life prior to your experiences of illness, because that would in effect deny and/or negate gains you have made in the process. We could stress this even more: your previous life and self do not exist any more. This last element speaks to the fact that recovery, in contrast to an absence of symptoms, relief from effects of illness or remediation of difficulties, often involves growth and expansion of the whole person.

Perspectives on recovery

The patient's perspective

In many ways, for a recovery journey to begin, there needs to be an acknowledgement that something needs to change. You may not even know what that is, you may not be able to verbalize or conceptualize it, but there is a belief that something, somehow, needs to be different.

> 'I am scared about what the future will be like, and I have no idea what it will be like, but I do know that I don't want to be where I am any more and that I can change things.'

There needs to be a belief that even though an eating disorder provides a sanctuary, a life full of illness means a severely compromised and unhappy future.

An eating disorder often convinces you that you are alone, that no one really understands what is happening, that the eating disorder behaviours and thoughts are the support system that keep you safe and secure. But nothing could be further from the truth. Family and friends may not understand the hold that the eating disorder has over you, but they do see the pain and distress. They have been through the painful process of seeing you disappear into a world full of rigidity and pain, helpless to pull you back despite their best efforts to do so.

With recovery, it is important that you are able to learn to listen to the people who love you the most and that you are able to begin to fight back against the voice inside your head. It is important for you to use the support to drown out the loud eating disorder thoughts. No one can battle an eating disorder alone. A team of specialist support is important, as is the presence of family and friends, to be a constant source of love and support and to remind you of the person you once were, the person who is trying to find their way back. Everyone experiencing an eating disorder needs love and support to guide them.

For many, the journey of recovery starts very gradually and the sense of loss that the illness has created is felt much more by the family around you rather than by you yourself. On many occasions you may really struggle to find the motivation to recover. To reach the stage of wanting to recover you sometimes have to detach yourself from the social and relational context around you, as you may have found them paralysing. Sometimes the recovery process can start with a separation from your family. This isn't necessarily a physical separation, but families have often described that through the illness experience they feel they have lost their loved one, and even when recovery has started, they do not always feel they are getting them back. Family members describe feeling disconnected and redundant, perhaps even rejected, unwanted and unloved. However, this disconnect may well be necessary for you to engage fully in a process that can aid your recovery, as it represents the separation that is needed to support the development of identity, which is critical for psychological well-being and independent functioning.

The search for identity is a critical developmental stage that typically takes place during adolescence, allowing a person to gradually move away from family ties to establish their own sense of being, which is linked to others but is independent from them. People with eating disorders are often struggling with this process, and this struggle is represented by the ambivalence that they feel towards the recovery process. On the one hand they want a quality of life back – this is often a tangible goal, such as returning to school, making plans for university, perhaps even a holiday or trip abroad, or making that career change they postponed for a long time. However, on the other hand their emotional well-being has been so overly dependent on the positive evaluation of others that they are not sure they exist in their own right outside of this. Therefore, these tangible goals become very frightening.

Making a decision to move away from the illness can thus feel very overwhelming. Many of you may feel a strong sense of guilt when you try to move away from the chains of the illness that keep you standing still. This is very difficult for families and carers to understand. The fact that motivation to recover changes constantly for you but is fixed for the family can create a fracture in the relationship, which can be very painful. The idea that on some days you may have a solid answer, a list of pros of recovery and cons of relapse, but then on other days the same answer might not feel enough any more, is very difficult for families and carers to understand. Sometimes you may need small tangible things to get through a day, like a supportive text message, and other days you may be able to focus on bigger things, like a conversation about an important subject. The families and carers don't always know which days are which, and this can be a constant source of confusion and fear, with the process of recovery sometimes feeling like a continuous journey with no clear road map and little sense of direction.

It is important for both you and your family to take into account all the different perspectives being held when you are talking together about what is happening, in order to manage the tension that this inevitably creates in your relationships. It is like you are speaking two different languages, and both parties feel misunderstood and at times not heard. What can be done in this situation is to explore and be interested in the perspectives of all those involved, even if hearing what the other person has to say causes a lot of distress.

Challenging an eating disorder provokes a myriad of difficult and painful feelings. Uncomfortable, complex emotions such as guilt, shame and regret are the weapons that an eating disorder uses to stop you from breaking free. In the midst of such feelings, you may be left experiencing a lack of control and power. It is at this point that it becomes very important to remember that these emotions, however intense and distressing, will not last forever. Feelings are temporary; they fluctuate and change moment by moment. They are difficult to predict and difficult to manage, but it is possible to overcome them. The more you can explore your thoughts and emotions, and challenge them when needed, the stronger you will become, and the easier things can become. Difficult thoughts and feelings can pass; even when in the moment it is hard to imagine that they will, it is important to believe that they can. Self-belief is a very important element in the recovery process, and it is not always easy to find after months, sometimes years, of being enslaved to a disorder that is life limiting.

It is important for you and also the people around you to acknowledge earlier on in the journey that recovery is not just about being able to regulate food choices safely, nor is it just about achieving a safe weight. This would only be a partial view of the recovery process as it does not take into account all the psychological and relational aspects. It also creates a false impression of recovery. For example, when you are able to eat a reasonable size meal, or to stop yourself from vomiting after a meal, or engaging in obsessive exercise to compensate for eating, it is not the end of the story. Assuming that can be very distressing for you in the recovery process, as it locates the eating disorder within the relationship to food, and does not account for the thoughts and feelings that fuel the behaviours. As thoughts and feelings are invisible and private, it is very difficult for those around you to see what is really going on, so an illusion can be created that all is well, when in fact the eating disorder thoughts and feelings can be stronger than ever.

Developing a healthy thought pattern regarding food, to be able to function competently around food and to be aware of how to manage potential triggers that may lead you to slip back, is an important part of recovery. Managing the negative feelings, though, is one of the hardest challenges of recovery. For some of you, these negative feelings may never fully go away, but for others, they may. The more distance created between you and the illness, the less frequent the thoughts become, and the easier it will be to engage in other aspects of life, moving you further away from the eating disorder. If this cycle can be maintained and reinforced it can take on a life of its own and replace the cycle of eating disorder thoughts, feelings and behaviours – a sign of recovery at a deep and significant level.

The family's perspective

Whilst an eating disorder reflects a complicated relationship with the self and is often caused by a unique combination of factors, such as genetics, environment and culture, family members can be a very powerful source of support through the recovery process. Family involvement cannot necessarily fix things, but the evidence base suggests that some forms of family intervention can be very effective and are a highly recommended treatment pathway for people with eating disorders. In adulthood it is recommended that family and partners are involved in treatment where possible. In many ways the family can hold the goal and hope for a happy and healthy life for the person when they are not always in a position to hold it for themselves.

Becoming a parent is a life-changing experience. From the moment the idea of a child is present in the parents' minds, they begin to imagine and build expectations about what that child might be like. They may imagine all sorts of things for their child: what they will look like, what they will be like, what type of dreams and aspirations they may have. So much love and time goes into these thoughts and feelings. However, what they never imagine is a child, young person or adult with an eating disorder. This means that all parents from the very start of the eating disorder journey are dealing with something they never anticipated and, even harder, something that is very difficult to understand. The first question they always ask is 'Why?' Sadly, there is not an easy answer to this question, but of course all parents need help to deal with supporting a person through an eating disorder, as eating disorders rarely resolve on their own, and it is also very difficult to avoid the illness having an impact on the entire family. It is important for all parents to remember that they did not cause the eating disorder, and they need support and care to help their child recover as well.

It is very hard for a parent or carer to understand how difficult it is to move away from a pattern of behaviours that are clearly destructive on a physical, social and emotional level. It is important to remember that the person trying to recover does not view the pattern of behaviours in the same way; instead they see it as a safe haven, as a sanctuary that keeps them safe from experiencing things that they might not feel able to manage. High levels of perfectionism and a strong self-critical attitude can make it challenging for you to believe that there could be anything different from the life you are experiencing in the moment. The pattern of behaviours that represent the illness have become your friend and you are fearful to let go, fearful of what change may bring. People around you may not understand this at all.

Acknowledging the need to recover from the illness is about engaging in the idea of developing a sense of identity that is free from the tyranny that the illness has created in your life. The degree to which you are aware of yourself as a separate self is dependent on the extent to which you have emerged from the family and to which the process of individuation has developed.

In terms of development, children and young people react not only to what adults say, but also to the implicit messages, values and expectations present in the surrounding environment. A child might be paid particular attention when they are obedient and quiet, or when they do things on their own without asking for help. The cause of the eating disorder is not to be sought only in the child as an individual, but also in their surroundings and their relationships with others, and the broader social context.

An eating disorder tends to freeze emotions and communication. The only conflicts that arise are around food and meals. As therapists, we often hear from family members that there have never been any previous problems. The person with the eating disorder was perhaps viewed as the easier child, the calmer adolescent or the competent young adult. In many instances their emotions have been suppressed and internalized: they never seem angry on the outside, but the internal distress develops into a pattern of emotion dysregulation, which causes suffering. The suffering causes emotional pain, psychological distress and the eating disorder behaviours.

Parents are generally ready to work towards recovery far sooner than the person experiencing the eating disorder. They may have noticed a gradual deterioration over many months; they may not have been aware of what exactly was wrong, but they knew that something was. They may have observed mood changes, behaviour changes around food, and social isolation and withdrawal. They may have noticed weight loss, weight gain, disrupted meals and frequent visits to the toilet after meals. Family tasks that once seemed pleasurable, such as going out for dinner, going for a picnic or even going for a coffee and snack, seem to have been replaced with anxiety and stress, if they are happening at all. Even though other family members may still enjoy these outings, the eating disorder becomes so powerful that it changes the behaviour of the whole family as it simply becomes too difficult. Food shopping and how this is managed also may have changed, with the person with the eating disorder showing more interest and wanting to have more control about what food choices are being made. Some may have stopped eating with the family completely, as mealtimes have become too difficult for them. Or mealtimes may have started to take up too much time, with the planning needed and then the time taken to consume the meal impacting on other areas of activities. As these changes are so gradual, parents do not necessarily realize how the family is generally accommodating so many changes. The degree of the problem can sometimes be spotted by someone outside of the family, like a friend or a teacher. Sometimes parents are able to piece it together, but it can be hard and there is often a degree of guilt and shame when parents feel they have missed changes that they should have noticed. For many parents this guilt and shame can be overwhelming.

It is important that parents access support to deal with this. Each and every family has many strengths, and it is important that the strengths are focused on, so the family can move through this process and recover as well. Guilt and shame are complex emotions that really don't benefit the recovery process at all, and it is important that in the first step of recovery this is acknowledged. Parents need to be able to let themselves off that big hook and think about what resources they have to support the person with the eating disorder. This is a very important step in the recovery process for the family, which is not stressed enough.

Within families, when a member is taken ill, the troops tend to rally. All family members may take on a role, be it taking care of the poorly family member, helping out more around the house, taking on responsibilities, and so on. The most effective way to manage the impact of an eating disorder in the family environment is to create a culture of compassion and warmth around aspects relating to food and body image, and to promote healthy balanced eating and body image in a positive, realistic and compassionate way. It is also important to become attuned to each other's emotions and acknowledge and validate them, even when it is hard to fully understand them.

At times when working with families, we come across parents with eating disorders, or who have had them in the past. There are many different forms this can take. The parent may be very open about this: they may take you to one side and explain that when they were growing up something similar happened. They may have accessed treatment, or they may have recovered over time alone. It is always helpful to know this as it provides a context for the family that is very real. Something that is perhaps more challenging to deal with is when a parent appears to have an eating disorder, but it is not acknowledged openly. It may be that as therapists we glimpse something in the values and attitudes that are shared in therapy. We may hear something that suggests the parent has an eating difficulty or perhaps another type of psychological illness. It is always important that over time, when the therapeutic relationship is secure and intact, some of these issues are aired in a gentle and supportive way. A parent-only session or a follow-up phone call may be offered, to create an opportunity for disclosure in private. Sometimes parents are not able to acknowledge their own struggle, or there is a degree of resistance. As therapists in these situations all we can do is try to be as compassionate as possible, but at the same time emphasize that each and every family member may need to do some work on themselves to improve the situation. On some occasions the therapist may be able to recommend a colleague who could offer a parent some individual support, and can suggest that this might feel beneficial, in the hope that this will help the parent engage with their own particular situation.

Remembering the needs of siblings

Recovery can be a long, slow process for all. While this can prove very challenging for parents, it is often the siblings who become the unnoticed victims of the illness. That is because parents understandably focus time, thought and energy onto the family member with the eating disorder. Whilst in the beginning this is accepted and understood as what needs to happen to enable recovery, over time siblings can feel overlooked and at times ignored. This is a very unhelpful dynamic, not just for the poorly child and the siblings but for the family system as a whole. The siblings have to find a way of being heard and seen. To do this they have to develop a louder voice. This can lead to the development of rebellious behaviours that will get them noticed. This is particularly challenging as no one in these scenarios is really in the wrong. The person with the eating disorder is struggling, the parents want to support them, and the other siblings need love and support too. This is why therapeutic approaches that can involve all family members can be very helpful in giving everyone a voice. When an eating disorder presents, whilst only one person may be unwell, the rest of the family can be at risk as well.

In the treatment of adolescents, siblings are often

included in the process of therapy. This is based on the idea that the eating disorder affects the whole family, and so the treatment also needs to pull on the strengths of the whole family. However, sometimes this is difficult, and after a few sessions siblings may become disinterested in the process. Furthermore, family therapy sessions may be at times that clash with school and other interests. Parents feel genuinely torn about how to approach this, as many appreciate the need to include the whole family but at the same time want to minimize the disruption to the other siblings' lives, which is of course understandable.

It is important that siblings are offered some form of education about the eating disorder. This information needs to be provided in a calm and contained way, ideally at a quiet time when the parent has had time to digest the information for themselves. It is important that the parent has had time to deal with their own feelings regarding this before attempting to share, because if the sibling senses a level of distress in their parent, this will be more stressful for them. At the same time, it is important that the parent can demonstrate that they are worried and concerned. So once again there needs to be a careful balance at a time of high stress for the parents.

How a sibling responds will be largely determined by their personality type. Children who are predisposed to anxiety may be upset and scared. They may also feel a sense of responsibility for the illness. Other, more laid-back children may be more accepting and less worried, emotionally held by their parent's response. Some siblings may experience frustration and anger. This can lead to feelings of guilt and thus internal emotional conflict. It is important that no sibling takes on a carer role, as this is too big for them to handle alone, and appropriate boundaries must be set so the sibling can support the person with the eating disorder appropriately and not take on too much.

> 'I used to feel really angry that my sister wouldn't eat and that every mealtime there was a big drama about it all. It felt like she was getting lots of attention for causing trouble. Later on, when I understood more about the illness, I felt really guilty for feeling this, it was really confusing.'

Of course, it is not possible to describe or clarify every type of response; it is about parents and carers knowing their child and trying to understand their response in the context of their personality. This can be difficult when the needs of the ill family member are so prominent.

As parents, it is important to remember the need of the siblings even when they seem to be getting on with everything okay. It is important that regardless of the illness and the impact this is having on the family routine, there are some norms that remain in place. Supporting the sibling to continue doing all the things that they find fulfilling is very important. Aspects that provide structure and safety are particularly important, such as school, friendships and social activities. This will give the sibling a sense of purpose and a sense that regardless of what is going on at home there are aspects of life that remain normal and unaffected.

For some siblings, the distress at seeing their parents so worried and concerned will be really upsetting. As a way of trying to support the situation they may try not to worry parents with their own needs and concerns, so as to ease the burden in some way. This is a really difficult situation for parents to manage, as they can then end up feeling that they may be failing their well child. It is important, where possible, for parents to demonstrate resourcefulness and an ability to cope. There may be moments when that isn't possible, but when this happens it is important for the parent to reflect with the child later and explain that it was just a difficult moment, a difficult day. It is important for parents to demonstrate that they are human too and that this is tough for everyone, but that as a family they can all move through this together.

Most of the discussion here has focused on the idea of growing up in a family where one of the children has an eating disorder. However, adults have eating disorders as well, which means that some adults are trying to cope with an adult sibling who has an illness. In many ways this is harder, as this situation isn't really talked about. Having a sibling with an illness at any age is devastating. Often, an adult sibling will have their own support system in the form of their own family outside of the family of origin. If the eating disorder has been present for a long period of time, there may be a degree of compassion fatigue. However, knowing that an eating disorder can limit the lifespan and cause premature ageing and health complications is something that takes on a greater importance in adult life. Again, compassion and understanding are very important issues to hold in mind when trying to support an adult sibling battling an eating disorder.

The involvement of partners and friends

Whilst eating disorders commonly develop around adolescence, they can also develop later in life, and some who struggle with an eating disorder in adolescence may carry that struggle into adulthood. In adulthood the support system around a person changes. Whilst in some instances parents are still involved, new people may also join the support system, such as trusted friends and partners. In some instances, the support systems become husbands, wives, partners, trusted friends and colleagues. The presence of the eating disorder can have an impact on the quality of these relationships. Within normal healthy relationships the level of need and demand changes from one person to another over time, depending on what is going on for that particular person. The balance in the relationship changes and there is a level of adaptation from each individual. A healthy relationship evolves flexibly through this process, and the individuals in the relationship find themselves adjusting accordingly. There is a general consensus that this is what a healthy dynamic relationship should be.

However, if your loved one develops an eating disorder, or continues to suffer from an eating disorder from adolescence into adult life, the balance can be very challenging to maintain. This is mainly because eating disorders can be very absorbing due to the fact that they are 'ego-syntonic'. Behaviours are defined as ego-syntonic when they seem to align with a person's goals, values and beliefs, so the person does not feel that they have to change them. All seems perfectly fine for them, or even if they know it is not fine, they do not think there is any need to change them. However, some people with eating disorders recognize that all is not right with their behaviour, and there may be aspects that they would like to change. The degree and extent of this awareness varies from individual to individual, and can improve throughout the treatment.

Take a few minutes to think about what it might be like

to be in a relationship with someone who is obsessed with food, whether it be restricting or purging. The problem with the obsession is that it begins to dictate all the terms and conditions of life, and in that sense nothing else feels as important. This is the aspect of an eating disorder that can seem very self-absorbed, and people with eating disorders can seem to be primarily occupied with their own thoughts and feelings above those of others. An eating disorder can also become all-consuming, but the partner in the relationship is often unaware of the extent of the problem. This is not because they are not observant and caring, but because people with eating disorders became very good at hiding just how difficult things really are. They can become an expert at denying the extent of the problem, even to themselves. They have a misperception of the quantity of food they are eating, so what partners and friends observe is different from what the person with the disorder reports.

If you are in a relationship with someone with an eating disorder, extend support and compassion to them but also hold in mind your own emotional needs as well. For a relationship to meet the needs of both people, there have to be not just shared interests but a shared mental space. However, if that space is not truly shared as one half of the relationship is preoccupied, the relationship can become unbalanced and unhealthy. Sometimes there may be an attempt to appear as if the mental space is shared, but this may not be as authentic as it needs to be and can lead to more complex problems within the relationship. If emotional and psychological needs are continually not met within a relationship, it can become detrimental to well-being.

Caring for someone with an eating disorder can put a strain on your own mental health; it is well known that eating disorders have a very high level of carer burn out. To try and avoid this, set boundaries; whilst you are supporting someone, you also have a life that has value and meaning. Remember that doing small things for yourself will help you to achieve that balance. Also, try to get support for yourself. This could be professional support, which can be very helpful, or simply sharing your stresses and strains with family and friends, even though this may at times be very difficult. This must not be seen as a breach of trust or betrayal; it is instead a way of strengthening the support system around the sufferer and is a key part of the recovery process.

Living with and tolerating uncertainty

Uncertainty about ourselves

Many of the people who we wrote to at the very beginning of the process of writing this book talked to us about uncertainty as a really important idea to think about. Some said they had come to terms with it, but for others it still yielded many challenges. At a certain point within the recovery journey, you may discover things about yourself that you value. Bringing you back to these things in therapy is important, and can help you to begin to tolerate the things you struggle to accept. Once this set of values becomes more established it can then be generalized to everyday decisions rather than just being applied to how you think about the world. For example, being kind may be a value that you hold dearly, and you always try to be kind. Generalizing on a broader level would mean that you value kindness from others towards yourself. Realistically, this is a step-like process that plays out in therapy. Initially you may struggle to find anything positive about yourself. In fact quite the opposite may be true: you may focus on everything you dislike about yourself. This can be very distressing for you and the loved ones around you. As you begin to reconnect with positive aspects of yourself, you may become better at tolerating the aspects that you struggle with. Once this is in place it can then be generalized from the therapy room to real-life situations that arise in your day-to-day interactions with the people in your life, and the general level of tolerance that you can manage gradually increases. This is very important, as the world is full of uncertainties and living with them is a human skill that is required to be able to thrive and prosper.

Uncertainty about our environment

From a biological, evolutionary perspective, our brains are wired to avoid and dislike uncertainty in our lives. This is because uncertainty creates anxiety, and we have set reactions for managing anxiety. From a survival perspective, when our brains perceive a threat or danger it will seek out information to either confirm or dismiss that threat. The brain will also assess the situation to evaluate the risk, in the hope that it can be avoided. In our brains, then, uncertainty represents less ability to avoid danger and, in that situation, thinking patterns are more likely to be catastrophic and full of fear. The natural state of the brain in relation to survival is to overestimate the risk to safety and underestimate the ability to tolerate uncertainty. Any increase in uncertainty then leads to an increased stress response, both from a neurological and physiological perspective.

When we think about eating disorder recovery, this

picture fits very well. Whilst life with an eating disorder can be miserable and unhappy, it can also feel predictable, safe and certain. There is often a day-to-day pattern or routine that keeps the person feeling safe and secure. This routine allows for no new challenges, no fears – there is almost a sense of contentment in the misery that keeps one safe. Life is predictable, safe and constant. However, when recovery enters into the picture, the dynamic changes. Just the thought of recovery and whatever that means can create a feeling of anxiety and uncertainty, let alone the thought of actually making any changes.

Recovery, in essence, represents change. Whether that be a change in eating patterns, a change in weight or a change in the way we think, that change generates anxiety. As already discussed, there is no easy way to recover, there is no road well-trodden, there is no size that fits all. It is an individual process – some therapies and approaches will work for some, other approaches may work for others. Some of you will choose to follow the path alone; others will involve loved ones. Nothing seems clear to you; everything feels scary, and nothing feels certain, and thus the certain predictable pathway of the eating disorder, although miserable, can feel safer and less risky.

However, what we have learnt about uncertainty over the years is that we are far more able to cope with uncertain situations than we believe ourselves to be. Thus the stress response to thinking about uncertainty can cause more anxiety than the actual situation itself. There is nothing as true as the statement 'there is nothing to fear more than fear itself'. This is why when we talk about engaging in eating disorder recovery, we need to acknowledge the idea of bravery, as someone embarking on this journey is indeed facing their worst fear – trying to manage the uncertainty that recovery creates. However, you may well find that once you start to walk down that particular pathway, the fear is not as bad as you had anticipated. Taking the first step is always the hardest. With eating disorder recovery, as with so many of life's challenges, we cannot remove the uncertainties – we can only walk alongside someone whilst they face them and be there for them.

So, living with the uncertainty becomes about finding a place for it in your life, in the same way you would for other issues that can't be resolved – again, the idea of acceptance leading to resolution. The more time spent challenging distressing thoughts, the hope is, the less frequent the thoughts become, so it begins to make sense that you can recover with time. But it is entirely possible that some aspects of the experience of having an eating disorder will always stay with you in some way. This may vary from one person to another.

In many ways, recovery is about making positive changes so that you can be successful in quietening down negative thoughts and not allow the eating disorder to hold all the power. It is important that recovery is represented realistically, as otherwise it can lead to a false sense of security, creating an impression that recovery can be complete, when really it is an ongoing process. Life can be full of ups and downs, and therapy and other treatment approaches do not eliminate these ups and downs from life. Instead, the process of therapy can enable you to manage these ups and downs without reverting to disordered eating habits. This is why it is more helpful to view recovery as an ongoing process rather than a task to complete.

For some, recovery can consist of a return to a healthy

weight, heightened awareness of your use of food to regulate emotions, and deep-rooted changes in your lifestyle. However, for others it can be less clear-cut. It can be about learning to accept tiny issues with food that sometimes aren't there and sometimes are. This may be related to food, but not always. It can be an unsettling feeling that is ever present but does not dictate or shape your food choices or your range of experiences within your life. Of course, everybody experiencing the pain of an eating disorder would prefer the first description of recovery, but the reality is that won't be everyone's experience, and it would be unrealistic to present it as such. Instead, for some, the process of recovery will be about a self-acceptance that a small part of this will be ever present, but that is okay, that is manageable and that does not interfere with life. That will be realistic recovery for some. The self-acceptance part is key, as it suggests that a comfortable position has been found, and this in itself is at odds with the distressing position that often accompanies disordered eating habits and eating disorders.

Often, we hear accounts from family members who are struggling to understand why their loved one cannot give up eating disorder symptoms, and continue to be resistant to the idea of therapy. It is at this point that we need to consider again the value of the symptoms. Whilst we view them as complicated obsessions that make life harder, you may not see it that way. Regardless of all the protocols, guidelines and scientific knowledge, we need to look beyond, we need to go once more to our knowledge and understanding of you as a person. We need to help you understand that your life can have meaning without the symptoms, and thus you will come to value the symptoms less. Recovery from an eating disorder requires attention to the whole human being in all their mental, emotional, physical, social and spiritual richness. It is not simply about helping you to eat again or not be afraid of your weight. It is helping you to move towards a new and different way of living or being in the world.

Good emotional well-being is achieved if human beings develop into full maturity according to the characteristics and laws of human nature. Mental illness consists in the failure of such development. We cannot treat the symptoms as if they are a box separate from the rest of our personality, and our vision for our future. We need to be able to understand what our beliefs and actions are that are contrary to our nature. If we live under conditions that are contrary to our nature and to the basic requirements for human growth and sanity, we cannot help reacting: we must either deteriorate and perish or bring about conditions that are more in accordance with our needs. We need to fully focus on ourselves, on our own being. We must be brave enough to face our challenges and be honest and open with ourselves, and then we will discover the opportunities treasured by our own life and the joy of living.

Chapter 6

What Happens in Therapy?

The process of psychological therapy is quite complex. Many authors and researchers have tried to describe it, to structure it, to evaluate it. In the field of eating disorders, we know very little about what the most effective therapy approaches are, and a great amount of research work continues to be conducted on this topic. Nonetheless, we are very confident about the fact that psychological therapy has a central role in the treatment of an eating disorder. However, it is one of the most difficult parts of the treatment to engage with, as it requires several fundamental components, such as a certain level of awareness in the person experiencing the eating disorder, the availability to open up about very personal issues to a professional, a degree of motivation towards change, and a lot of patience, as change requires some time.

It would be impossible here to describe the whole process of therapy, so we have chosen to touch upon some of the most important aspects related to it. We provide a brief description of a theoretical model that can help you to break down the process of recovery into steps, so it can feel a little less overwhelming. We talk about the possibilities of starting therapy at different stages of the recovery process and with different degrees of motivation. We also report on the common questions related to the relationship with the therapist and the main themes discussed throughout the sessions. We hope that this information may give you more confidence in asking for psychological support.

The therapeutic process: A circular pathway

'I keep telling my daughter that she needs help, but she cannot even see the problem, and we fight about it all the time. It is too hard seeing her destroying herself. I cannot just sit and watch.'

'We have been in therapy for a few years now. We attended all the groups, read all the books. You have seen him every week, and yes, he is physically better now, but he continues to eat, what, four or five different meals? Is that all we can hope for? Food will continue to be like a monster for him?'

'I am ready to start therapy now. How long will it last? I am used to doing everything on my own, so now I am here I know I have to be consistent, and you have to keep me accountable, and don't believe me when I tell you that I am better – keep asking me.'

We are sure that these views may sound familiar to many of you. At times the therapeutic and the recovery pathway can feel very bumpy, and this can lead to feelings of uncertainty and despair. We can tell you with conviction that recovery from an eating disorder is fully possible, but it is not an easy journey for anyone, and it is not one you can take on your own. There are many research studies that have looked at the recovery outcomes, and the general consensus is that those who are engaged in a treatment process tend to do better than those who are not.

When working with people who have had lifelong battles, we have found that they often haven't accessed treatment for a number of years, and have for the best part suffered in silence and experienced a degree of shame through their lifetimes. Being able to acknowledge their struggle through the process of therapy can be very helpful and, in some instances, they are able to tackle their eating disorder in a way that they never thought possible. Often for this group, the eating disorder has not dominated their life but has been something that has always been present. As a result of this, they often talk about their life lacking a sense of authenticity as they have struggled to open up in relationships, or they have talked about always holding something back.

When we think about this as therapists, it is a very sad thing that someone's life is blighted in this way, when if they had accessed support sooner things could have been very different. This is why it is so important that body image and eating disorder issues are talked about openly from an early age, that appropriate treatments are available, and that you are able to take this brave step forward and engage in recovery.

Another common question asked when talking about recovery is how long it can take. Again, there are no straight-forward answers. Research suggests that recovery can take anywhere between six months and six years, and is dependent on different factors, such as duration of illness, severity of symptoms, ease of access to treatment, and other more individual factors such as level of motivation to make the necessary changes. When trying to manage this uncertain process, it can be helpful to take a very flexible approach to what the therapeutic steps and recovery can look like. As discussed in the previous chapter, taking a fixed view of recovery may lead to disappointment and frustration, but viewing the therapeutic process and recovery more as a series of stages that can be moved through may help you to understand why this process can be so lengthy, and help create a sense of momentum even when you don't feel that you are progressing. So keeping the idea of recovery as a possibility is very important, and holding a stage-like process in mind can help to provide a framework for maintaining this.

The stages of change model

The stages of change model is one of the main models used in psychology to describe the steps that people usually go through when they are thinking about changing their behaviours.[1] This model looks at how people change unwanted behaviours, and was originally used to help people overcome problematic behaviours like alcohol and drug abuse, overeating and smoking. It is extensively applied in eating disorders as a framework to help people identify where they are at in regard to how they see the eating disorder and their motivation towards change. This model is also used to discuss with people and their families what treatment goals it would be helpful to prioritize and focus on, based on the stage identified.

The model is interesting because it presents change as a

cycle rather than a linear process. It describes five stages of change through which people pass through whilst trying to make a change: precontemplation, contemplation, preparation, action and maintenance.

The precontemplation stage is the point where you may not believe that you have a problem. Your family and friends may notice behaviour changes around food, such as restrictive eating or a binge/purge cycle, or a preoccupation with weight, shape and appearance, before you are able to admit it. At this stage you may refuse to discuss the topic and become quite hostile when it is mentioned. In terms of what can be supportive at this point, you may be more open to gentle discussion than full-on facts and figures about eating disorders. The conversation needs to be gentle and tentative, with no clear answers being presented as facts. It is important that the family member or friend is not in denial about the extent of the problem. They need to be aware of the signs and avoid falling into the trap of rationalizing your problematic behaviours. This is easily done, as you may be very convincing when you deny you have any difficulties. They need to openly share their thoughts and concerns with you.

The contemplation stage occurs when you are willing to admit that you have a problem and are now open to receiving help. The fear of change may be very strong, but something within you has shifted to being able to accept the idea of seeking some help. At this point professional help can be very meaningful, as it can support you and your family to begin to think about what purpose the eating disorder is serving for you and why it is currently in your life. This in turn can help you move closer to making changes.

Next comes the preparation stage, when you are ready to

change but are uncertain how to do it. As part of this it can be helpful to explore your own thoughts and beliefs about food, weight, shape and appearance. Often in therapy, time is spent establishing specific ways of dealing with negative eating disorder thoughts and emotions, and ways to tend to your own self-nurture needs. At this point it is also usual to think about things that might get in the way of making changes so that strategies can be put in place to try and manage this as well. From a supportive perspective, it can be helpful at this point for family members and friends to think about what role they can play in this process, to support you to implement the changes.

The action stage begins when you are ready to implement strategies and confront the eating disorder behaviour head on. At this point, you are more open to trying new ideas and behaviours and are willing to face fears in order for change to occur. This may involve following advice from professionals, and removing barriers to change and connections to unhelpful aspects of behaviour patterns that might trigger more eating disorder thoughts and feelings. For example, rather than choosing restaurants where you know the calorie content of the meals, which may take you back to a time when you needed to know this, you may choose a restaurant new to you. Or you may choose not to have certain conversations with some of your peers as you know that these can heighten your own anxiety and make you feel vulnerable to eating disorder thoughts and feelings.

The maintenance stage evolves when you have sustained the action stage for a period of time. Within the maintenance stage, you actively practise new behaviours and new ways of thinking as well as consistently using healthy self-care and coping skills. Part of this stage also includes revisiting potential triggers in order to prevent relapse, establishing new areas of interests, and beginning to live your life in a meaningful way.

The stages of change model is a very useful approach to help you understand how change can happen and what may get in the way. It also offers a very helpful therapeutic tool to help you think about what you need to move from one stage to another. It provides a framework that helps you to understand the challenges and why it may feel so hard to move forward.

You may go through this cycle more than once or may need to revisit a particular stage before moving on to the next. You may also go through the stages for each individual eating disorder symptom. For example, if you are recovering from anorexia nervosa, you could be in the action stage for restrictive eating, and eating three meals a day along with snacks, engaging in social eating and utilizing support systems to help you whilst, at the same time, you could be going through the contemplation stage for body image and weight concerns, becoming aware of how body image is tied to self-esteem and self-worth, defining oneself as a number on a set of weighing scales or a set of measurements, and identifying the negatives of striving for the 'perfect body'.

If you are trying to recover from bulimia nervosa you may be in the action stage, trying to eat regular meals and snacks to balance your blood sugars, but weight fluctuations may distress you, and you may slip back to the precontemplation stage of believing that this is not really a problem, as when you engage in a bulimic pattern of behaviour your weight is more stable, which is easier to manage from an emotional perspective. Whilst this is a distorted thought pattern it will reduce anxiety and thus becomes very reinforcing.

It will also fit with very fixed core beliefs that you gain weight quicker than anyone else, that weight shows on you more than others, and all sorts of other distressing cognitions tied to unhelpful and maladaptive core beliefs about weight and body size.

Both these examples demonstrate precisely why recovery from an eating disorder is complex and needs to be individualized. It is very difficult to change behaviours that fulfil such a specific purpose in your life, and this is a common experience for people with an eating disorder. For family members and friends, who may not have insight into the thought processes they go through, it can be very confusing and frustrating. They may see the level of commitment on the one hand, but not understand the change that occurs and the shift in commitment. It may be very difficult for you as the person with the eating disorder to be truly transparent about your thoughts due to shame, guilt and despair. This reinforces the sense of emotional and social isolation and can make the eating disorder stronger, at times creating a resistance and fear of recovery.

The stages of change model can be a very helpful framework for helping you to conceptualize the recovery process. At times of great uncertainty and despair it can reduce your anxiety and help maintain a level of hope and belief that recovery can continue and the bumps, even the big bumps, in the road are part of the process, and that it is okay to feel despair.

In reality, when you are struggling with recovery, it may feel quite hard to think about the model; at these times it might be easier for the family members and friends around you to hold it in mind. When talking to our patients about the stages of change model they have often struggled to think about the maintenance stage. They feel that perhaps there shouldn't be an end stage to the model, that maintenance isn't simply continuing to recover and maintain the changes whilst managing any setbacks, but should be a more open and fluid stage that is continuous. This is an interesting and thoughtful observation and is perhaps more realistic in terms of what you experience.

The initial phase of therapy

The stages of change model might make it less difficult to understand why you, along with many others, experience many conflicting emotions when contemplating seeking out therapeutic support. Your difficulties may have been going on for many years; you may have thought about reaching out before, but never quite made it over the line to turn the idea into any form of reality. There may be many emotions that push you from a precontemplative state to something more, but the need for understanding is something that seems to resonate with most people when they walk into the therapy room.

For some, it may be something very recent in their lives that has led to them seeking support, such as a new relationship or a new role in life. For others, the desire to understand their eating disorder has been present for many years, but it is only now the right time. Sometimes the emphasis in life can change, and that can create a space where things that have been put off can be thought about. What has brought people to this point is not clear either to us as therapists or the patient themselves. It can be different reasons for each and every one of you, and some may not even know.

117

However, as therapists we are curious about this, and one of the first questions we ask ourselves is 'Why now? What has brought this patient into our lives at this point in time?' This heralds the start of us thinking about you, your life and your needs in relation to us.

Making a start: Internal motivation

The initial sessions with Judith are a good example of how therapy might begin, and the main issues that are important to explore at the beginning of the therapy process. When she first contacted me (Lucia) to ask about the possibility of starting therapy, she wrote:

> *I am approaching a milestone with regard to my illness. I found you on the internet and thought your website looked interesting. I am not currently unwell.*
>
> *During my reading of some of the research, lots of things seem to fall into place. I want to understand more. I feel like sometimes it is still there even though I am not unwell. When I am struggling with stress the behaviours can come back. I am keen to understand more.*

I felt that she wrote that email with an open heart. I saw her determination in researching a scientific explanation for her eating disorder. She wanted to specify that she was fine, maybe meaning that her physical health was not compromised and she did not require urgent medical treatment. I supposed that in the past she may have had intensive treatment involving dietary and medical input aimed at containing the physical impairment. I thought that maybe at that time she did not feel completely ready to overcome the eating disorder.

It can take great tenacity to research scientific explanations for an eating disorder. At times when physical health is compromised, medical treatments are necessary. However, whilst this intervention can help prevent or contain the physical deterioration so often characteristic of eating disorders, it does not always help with understanding the meaning of symptoms. It is also true that at times treatment for eating disorders is imposed because of the physical risk, even when the person doesn't feel ready. This often reinforces their fear of receiving help and builds a wall between the person with the eating disorder and carers.

We quickly scheduled a first meeting. Judith was a bright 30-year-old successful woman. I invited her to speak freely about her difficulties, needs and expectations from psychological therapy. She analytically described the milestones of the development of anorexia nervosa throughout her life. She gave a detailed account of all the treatments received, and succinctly summarized her family dynamics. It seemed like she had told that same story so many times that she had become detached from it.

'I am anxious all the time and incredibly tired. But, if nothing has changed in all these years, surely it can't change now. There must be something wrong in me. Please, tell me so.'

I suggested that perhaps instead of focusing on what might be wrong, we could start focusing on understanding better her needs behind the eating disorder.

'This is scary. I don't know what my needs are. I am like a puppet, programmed to respond to others.'

'Maybe this is why you are here. We will get to know Judith together.'

Judith shared a dream in one of the initial sessions, when we were exploring the expectations and doubts she had about therapy. Independently from the therapeutic approach used by the therapist, dreams can always bring good insights on what the person might be experiencing in that moment of their life. They use images and storytelling which help to convey the emotional experience. They can appear bizarre or weird, but they can often be a helpful tool to start addressing important themes. Therefore we welcome them, and we are keen to hear about them.

Judith said that in the dream she found herself on a beach. It was dark, but not enough to prevent her from seeing the force of the sea crashing on the shore. Why was she there? She could not remember. She has always loved the sea, bewitched by its impelling power. A knot in her gut tensed her whole body every time she was in front of something mysterious and appealing at the same time. The sea was one of these things.

A little lively blonde girl shook her from her stillness with an open smile. She took Judith's hand and dragged her down the beach. Judith was surprised by her flowing energy. How could she be so serene and confident in that deep night? She pointed at some spots on the sand and told Judith that they had to dig them up. Judith's belongings were waiting for her, under the sand.

As soon as they started, Judith pulled out all sorts of

objects and body parts. The more she took out, the more they kept emerging from the sand. It was difficult to identify them; some were scary, others grotesque. The girl was peacefully standing close to her, attempting to reassure her by smiling and nodding.

We made sense of this dream by reflecting on the idea that there were important things that had been buried for a long time, and the need for support to unearth them. In her dream Judith was walking in the safety of the beach, guided by a warm-hearted child, but at the same time she was encouraged to approach and explore the depth of what was experienced on the surface as familiar.

'I guess you will help me to see all the things I tried to hide under the sand throughout all these years. But am I the frightened woman or the kind girl? Maybe both.'

In fact, we thought that the child could represent the vital and determined part of her, which was sacrificed throughout the years of the illness.

We chose the example of Judith to show that the treatment and recovery process consists of different phases, which are not always synchronized. As part of inpatient and outpatient treatment, Judith had had therapy in the past, but she felt that she had not truly engaged, as the motivation to recover was coming more from her family at that time. She had also understood that it was important she kept herself safe from a physical point of view, and she had agreed to engage in the medical and nutritional side of the treatment. She had learnt coping strategies to manage the invasive thoughts about food and weight and not act on them. However, the obsessions about food and body image, the anxiety, the perfectionism were still there, and she had never asked herself in the past what the internal and external factors were that kept these aspects going.

Therapy can therefore have different functions and goals at different stages in life. These are usually explored in the initial sessions with both you and your family or loved ones.

Making a start: External motivation

When people are ill, they are often brought to us. You, as the person with the illness, may not always see the necessity. You do not see things as a problem – it is everyone around you who holds that view. Some of you are willing, some are reluctant and some are resistant. This brings up an aspect relevant to the therapy process: the fact that, for many of you, your relationship with a therapist is not one that is chosen by you, rather one that is imposed on you. Even in adult services, whilst the pressure to engage in therapy can be different, where an adult has more say, there can still be external pressure from family members or healthcare professionals that pushes a person into something they do not feel ready for.

You may not be ready to begin the therapeutic relationship, yet therapy is being advised. This leaves the people around you in a paradoxical situation where they know it is important, but they can't seem to engage you in the idea. Therapy is being talked about as being very important for treatment and recovery, but it becomes almost impossible to manage the challenge when you can't see the point of talking, or even attending a session. Alternatively, you may take the opposite approach: you see therapy as another task to achieve well in, to be perfect in, and so it almost morphs into another representation of the illness. When an encounter is imposed, it can't always be a relationship, as a relationship needs to be chosen by both people involved.

If you are a young person, your parents might be asking you to attend the sessions, but you don't feel ready. In this situation, we would encourage you to give it a go anyway, at least for a few sessions, and discuss with the therapist what you might feel ready to address right now. This will allow you to express your views and needs, and the therapist can help you to communicate them to your family. Maybe we can use the time to observe together what is happening and what has changed in the past few months, and try to understand why your parents are worried for you and have contacted a therapist. Even if you don't feel the need to change anything, perhaps you are curious to know more about the thoughts and emotions you are experiencing. If you feel that your parents are worried about your eating and weight, whilst you are concerned about other things that are happening or have happened in your life with your friends, school or family, we could explore those. No one can make you engage in therapy if you don't feel ready, but trying to explore your feelings about it with your parents and the therapist may help you, and also enable them to help and guide you in a way that you find supportive.

If you are an adult, it might be easier to have a direct and open conversation with the therapist about your position on accessing therapy. Whether you have been encouraged by your family or partner to start therapy, or you have your own personal motivation, it will be important to talk about this at the beginning so that professionals can personalize the sessions for your needs.

For many, the experience of engaging in therapy can

come much later than the acute stage of illness. For some this will be weeks or months, for others it may be a period of years, and for others still, this time never comes. Many of you will want to reach this stage more quickly than you actually do. You may want to be rid of the symptoms more quickly than the process of safe recovery allows. Whilst this rush is understandable, it is important to take the time to engage in the process as this will ensure a safe and maintainable recovery. It is difficult to know what actually motivates a person to reach this significant point in their lives. Most commonly it is the aligning of some key factors which leads to a 'tipping point' of change, at which the balance finally tips in favour of pursuing recovery as opposed to continuing with the illness. For some, this seems to be one discrete moment in time; for others, it is experienced as a series of moments.

Timing

In order to be effective, therapy needs a consistent time and space, which can represent a still point, where the process of life can just be paused and reflected on in terms of meaning and value. Families often get upset if you skip a session, or in their keenness for you to recover, they ask for more and more sessions and interventions. Therapy is not like a medication that will have more effect if we increase the dose. In fact, for therapy to be truly effective it cannot just take place in 50-minute sessions. The therapeutic work consists of the flux of reflections, introspections and actions that occur not only in the consulting room with the therapist but also between the sessions. The realization of how long this journey can be and how much hard work it can involve may be overwhelming. However, what will make the greatest difference will be the quality of the relationship you build with your therapist.

Aspects of the therapeutic relationship

Can therapists cure an eating disorder?

As therapists, we are commonly asked if we are able to cure an eating disorder. The answer is not always clear, but we do believe that our willingness and openness to connect with you emotionally and intuitively, and to support you to discover the story or stories behind your symptoms, are key parts of the journey. We are not able to make promises about recovery, and we are not always able to provide timeframes that can then be evaluated later. We can offer a relationship based on the understanding that a therapeutic relationship, just like any relationship, develops over time and it is the essence of that development that becomes important to the recovery. It is your motivation that is key, and regardless of the therapeutic approach, if you allow yourself to be open to the therapeutic relationship, this will help you to understand what recovery means for you.

What is the most effective therapy approach?

We are also often asked about the effectiveness of psychotherapy over other approaches. We cannot reply unequivocally to this question. Therapy is different in every case. Sometimes people with eating disorders can have unhelpful therapy experiences. It often seems that when the treatment is delivered with you as an active participant, you have more opportunity to be involved and make a difference in your treatment. You should be offered therapies that are as individualized as possible, because the solution of the problem is always an individual one. A solution that may be out of the question for you may be just right for someone else. Therapy is a dialogue demanding two partners. The therapist sits facing you, you are eye to eye; the therapist has something to say, but so do you.

How can a therapist understand me if they have never experienced an eating disorder?

In addition to theoretical knowledge and clinical expertise, there are many qualities and skills that will support the therapist in the process of developing an understanding of your experience. Warmth, gentleness and compassion immediately spring to mind. However, a therapist also needs to have clarity of thought and be able to be firm and clear at times. Another important factor in understanding you is the importance of the therapist understanding themselves. That is not to say that a therapist has the world sorted and experiences no problems or difficulties. On the contrary, what type of therapist who breezes through life would really be able to empathize with distress and pain? It is important that the therapist has some understanding of their own weaknesses and how their own difficulties impact on them so they can contain their own emotional responses to any emotion expressed by you. For therapy to be effective a close rapport is needed, so the therapist must be open to the pain and suffering but not party to it.

A good therapist will hold a combination of clinical

expertise and have good interpersonal skills which respond empathically to your explicit and implicit experiences and concerns. Research suggests that sensitivity and flexibility in the use of therapeutic interventions produces better outcomes than rigid application of principles, and of course this makes perfect sense: it is not just a case of what you are doing but also a case of how you are doing it. Sensitivity is defined as being susceptible to the attitudes, feelings or circumstances of others, registering very slight differences or changes of emotion. In many ways, this sensitivity is akin to a musical instrument, which must be carefully prepared, maintained, tuned and protected. The clinician's capacity for intersubjective communication depends upon them being open to intuitive sensing of what is happening behind the patient's words and, often, in the back of their conscious awareness.[2]

Sensitivity and emotional intelligence are key for both the therapist and for you. You may have developed psychological symptoms because you are sensitive to implicit messages, emotional nuances and contradictions. The therapist is able to understand what is not said, to do what is expected even when it is not asked of them. In many instances the therapist has to understand the workings of the family and also inform their thinking from both social and cultural expectations.

In our view therapy only begins after the investigation of the whole personal story. It is your secret, the rock against which you are shattered. The therapist's task is to find out how to gain that knowledge. In therapy the problem is always the whole person, never the symptoms alone. We must ask questions that challenge the whole personality.

Human relationships are central to the therapeutic experience. The main therapeutic task is to help you in your search for autonomy and self-directed identity by evoking awareness of your impulses and feelings, and the needs that originate within you. The therapeutic focus needs to support you to understand your difficulties with how you see yourself, to understand the challenges that defective tools and concepts for organizing and expressing needs can lead to.

As we understand it, in eating disorders, poor attunement leads to an attitude of mistrust towards the body, its stimuli and its needs. Therapy represents an attempt to repair the conceptual defects and distortions, the deep-seated sense of dissatisfaction and helplessness, and the conviction that your own self is empty and incomplete and that therefore you are condemned to compliance out of helplessness. The emphasis has to be on listening to you and stimulating curiosity and sensitivity towards yourself. This active exploration in fact leads to improvement in the psychological state.

It is therefore essential for the therapist to show humility and inquisitiveness and acknowledge that we cannot know for sure what is actually happening in your mind. The therapist must be authentically interested and curious in exploring with you so they can model the idea of possibilities and hopefully stimulate you to be more curious about your own internal world, and to enable you to connect up to this internal state as a true representation of yourself, rather than the state you have constructed based on other people's evaluation of you. In this way, it is possible for you to develop trust towards yourself again.

Therapy as a mutual relationship

The idea of choice may be a new experience to you, as this might not be something that has been common to your experience of emotional connections in the past. Whenever the clinical setting allows, introducing the idea of choice from the beginning suggests that the relationship is about two human beings, independent and separate from one another, but that at the same time these two people are choosing to develop a meaningful relationship. Something about the act of choosing empowers an individual to feel comfortable with themselves. Focusing and prioritizing your own needs and making choices according to them can still be a frightening experience, though, as we described above in the vignette about Judith.

Therapeutic interventions provide an opportunity to experience a mutual relationship, where value and identity can be acknowledged. For a relationship to be truly mutual, it needs to allow and encourage the development of the other person's autonomy, otherwise it would become a co-dependency, or a sadomasochist dynamic where one is on a pedestal and the other feels inferior. Mutuality does not always include symmetry or equality. For example, a teacher and a student may have mutual admiration for each other without thinking that the quality or quantity of their admiration is identical, and that their roles and functions are symmetrical.[3] This view discards the idea that the therapist has superior knowledge of the patient's mind. The therapeutic space is instead seen as a creative space where the meaning is constructed together. The therapist is a participant in the therapeutic encounter, far more than just an observer.

The ability to engage in a relationship with another demonstrates to you as the patient that you can build true and deep connections with others, even though this can be challenging at times in the course of therapy. Reflecting on the dynamics that occur within the therapeutic relationship is in itself part of the work, and provides the opportunity to understand better the characteristics of the relationships you have in your personal life.

For example, if you find yourself tending to please other people and prioritizing their needs, it can be automatic to do the same with your therapist and play the role of the 'perfect patient'. This is something that will be explored and discussed in the sessions. One of the goals of therapy will then be starting only as yourself, without the intention to please others or your therapist. In this way the therapy journey becomes about dedicating a space only to yourself, a completely personal space, a space to tell your own story, to find a meaning that makes sense to you and maybe only you. The story can be told over and over again, but it is only when someone truly listens to the story that ownership can begin, and a sense of identity can be found.

In your life you may have experienced difficult relationships, whereby you felt the need to control others, or you felt controlled and unable to express your needs. In these cases, developing trust is a slow and anxiety-provoking process. Accepting help may be experienced as self-indulgent, making you feel needy, weak or selfish. Emotional self-sufficiency becomes highly desirable, and you feel the need to prove over and over again to yourself that you can exist in isolation, that you can manage alone, that meaningful connections should be limited for fear of exposure. It is important to talk openly about these fears in the sessions so you can explore and challenge them, preventing them from disrupting the therapeutic process, and allowing you to progress in your recovery.

What do we talk about in therapy?

Wilfred Bion, an influential English psychoanalyst, pointed out that in the therapy room both the patient and the therapist are somewhat two frightened people, and this tension is what will lead them to find out something new.[4] Many conversations will be held throughout the therapy sessions, and none of these will be easy or straightforward. The therapist will feel challenged by your questions and rewarded when their input is helpful. You might feel vulnerable as well, sometimes supported and understood as never before, other times disappointed again by someone who cannot provide definite and quick solutions. Despite this, it is important that both the therapist and you are able to share your thoughts about what would feel helpful to talk about. At the beginning, the therapist will have some main questions that they will ask, to give them an overview of your background history, and your current difficulties and resources. After that, based on your needs and previous therapy experiences, together you will decide where to start from. There is no right or wrong. All themes are important, and you will realize that they are all connected to each other.

We can simplify the process by summarizing the main aspects to consider as three major themes: eating disorder *symptoms*, *meaning* and *identity*.

Through one cycle of therapy, or more cycles of therapy conducted at different stages, it would be important that you reflect on your eating patterns, the thoughts and emotions you have about food, your body, any behaviours that impact on your body such as exercising and self-harm, and so on. This theme is therefore related to understanding and monitoring the specific eating disorder symptoms and to understand what actions need to be taken to manage any risks to your safety and physical health. Initially the focus will be more on the present. You will see that symptoms tend to repeat themselves and form a vicious cycle, which initially seems to offer protection and a sense of predictability, but then makes you feel more and more trapped and in physical and emotional pain. What are the actions that can be taken at this stage to break or change the cycle a little?

It would then be also helpful to explore how your relationship with food and your body developed over the years. This leads us towards the second theme: taking the gaze beyond the symptoms by exploring the emotional, social, cultural and relational meanings they have in the wider context of your life. We often say that every person with an eating disorder shows exactly the same symptoms, but manifest those symptoms to express different and very personal needs. As we have already said in Chapter 3, the eating disorder is not just about food, but about how you use food to communicate your emotions, to regulate the distance from other people, or to say something about your identity. This leads us towards the third theme. As we said, recovery does not simply mean overcoming the symptoms, but also developing a broader and deeper understanding of yourself as a person. It is therefore very important to explore the underlying personal characteristics that are maintaining the eating disorder, and that, if expressed differently, could lead towards a more fulfilling life.

Obviously, therapy needs to be relevant to your life. The more you are open to talking about yourself, reporting examples of what happens in your day-to-day life and sharing your reflections of yourself, the more the therapist can support you with finding new perspectives and ways to express yourself.

In the paragraphs below we share more thoughts on these main themes, being mindful of the fact that we are addressing only at a surface level the meaningful and personal conversations that we share in the sessions.

From managing the eating disorder symptoms...

Whenever we face a physical or mental health difficulty, the healthcare systems help us to observe and monitor the symptoms, and provide guidance on how to manage them, ideally to a point where they do not impact on life functioning and do not limit life experiences. They also develop an understanding of the illness by observing interconnections between various factors such as genetic, biological, social and psychological factors. This approach is very helpful in terms of developing a big picture of the illness, shaping treatment programmes and interventions. At a psychological level, this translates into therapy by collecting information about behaviours, thoughts and emotions that are related to eating and your relationship with your body. From a therapeutic point of view, psychoeducation plays a key role at this stage. Psychoeducation can be defined as a learning experience about oneself. It can focus on the process or the symptoms you are suffering from and the best way of coping with the consequences of such a disorder. The use of psychoeducation needs to be collaborative and seeks your active participation in talking about what is scientifically known about your symptoms. Once we have shared the understanding and the knowledge we have about the symptoms, then we can think together how to manage them, focusing on decreasing the food preoccupations, and developing awareness on to what extent your self-worth is defined by the weight and shape of your body. This initial phase can be very difficult and complex as there are times when the clinical interventions need to focus promptly and prescriptively on saving a life or preventing long-term harm. In these moments the illness is very vivid and alive.

On many occasions, family members have shared the distress and pain of talking to their child and hearing them only asking questions or talking about food in a repetitive way that seems very irrational and illogical. At moments like these, you and your family may talk about the symptoms in completely opposite ways. You don't see any of your behaviours as symptomatic or risky, and you do not associate them with illness, whilst your family shares their despair as they do not know how to connect with you and help you to change your behaviours.

Eating disorder symptoms present so many conflicts for young people and adults, parents and carers, and the professionals and systems around them. Why do these symptoms present in the way they do? And how do we manage them? Parents and carers want to understand why their child can't eat, why it takes them so long, why they will eat only certain foods, why they won't let anyone else prepare their food. The number of concerns and worries is endless, and one set of behaviours appears to lead to the development of other behaviours, or one set of behaviours can disappear, to the relief of parents and carers, only to be replaced by another set of behaviours that may be as concerning, or even more concerning. This is a source of great anguish for people caring for a loved one with an eating disorder.

Despite the countless concerns of the people around you, you might have had the sensation at the onset of the illness that you were feeling better about yourself, especially when you were able to control food. At times you might even have felt superior to others because through your tenacity and dedication you were able to do something that others couldn't: you could control food, at least for a certain period of time. The urge to control food is present in any kind of eating disorder. This period can be described as the honeymoon period, and most people, wherever they are in their recovery process, describe the beginning of the eating disorder as something that made them feel good, giving them a sense of achievement or protection. Initially, both the physical and the psychological negative consequences are underestimated, and barely noticed.

This initial lack of awareness of the negative impact that the illness has on your body and mind, and the focus on the apparent positive side of the eating disorder, is very painful and disorientating for the families and carers involved in your care and support, as they find it difficult to understand and they don't know how to communicate with you. We see the disorientating pain of the families lost in the apparently unintelligible intricacies of the symptoms.

In this initial phase, you may well struggle to perceive and control accurately bodily sensations such as hunger and satiety, fatigue and weakness as the physiological signs of malnutrition, and pain. This provides a sensation of disembodiment, whereby the body is emotionally and cognitively experienced more via external concrete feedback such as weight scales, measuring limb circumferences and counting skin folds on the stomach. Also, identifying emotional states clearly represents a challenge; you may not have the language to be able to reflect on and express the way you are truly feeling, and may really struggle to identify any feelings.

When it is difficult to perceive and understand the emotional and physiological internal reality, the body as an object to control and measure assumes a central role in giving a sense of continuity and order to the self. The body literally becomes a body of evidence. The manifest symptoms essentially serve the function of maintaining the cohesion and stability of a tenuous sense of self.[5] Food restriction provides a sense of purpose. Living and experiencing life is put on hold until this goal is met. However, the goal is never truly met as it continually moves; as you reach your initial goal, the pleasure and sense of achievement you feel ensure that you relentlessly pursue the next goal, and so on and so on. The illness and suffering provide a fulfilling meaning in life, but it is a solution that can destroy the experience of living.

It is of course very important from a physical perspective that these symptoms and behaviours are managed at a stage like this. In an inpatient setting, various creative care plans will be developed to support you to manage your symptoms. In outpatient settings parents and carers are taught methods to manage these difficult behaviours so they can support you to avoid an inpatient admission. The creative work, energy, simple dedication and love that goes into managing symptoms is completely astonishing.

And in many instances, it is lifesaving and life changing. The level of professional skills needed to manage a person with an eating disorder should not be underestimated, and neither should the level of love and determination shown by families all around the globe trying to support their family member to combat this devastating illness.

In this initial phase we share our knowledge of the eating disorders with parents and carers, and support them in understanding the manifestations of the illness and tolerating the suffering that comes from it. At the same time, we try to help you to develop awareness of unhelpful behaviours related to food and your body, and understand and accept that these are a sign of the fact that you are suffering. Once we reach an agreement about this, we can then start thinking about what the function and the meaning of these symptoms in your life might be.

...to searching for meaning

We are in fact often asked the question: Why? Why did this happen to me? Why did this happen to my child? There is no straightforward answer, and a deeper understanding can only be achieved together. In life we often search for meaning, and our quest for meaning becomes ever more intense when we can't understand why things happen. In many ways, perhaps it is the search that distracts us from the pain of different life traumas. If we can't find meaning we often feel at a loss, and we struggle to cope and make sense of experiences. A lack of meaning, or our struggle to find meaning, often affects how we cope. Meaning helps us cope with emotional experiences, and as a result our search for meaning to help us understand our lives and experiences is continuous.

It is important to acknowledge and understand that from a psychological perspective, the worry and preoccupation with food, weight and body image is a disguise used to cloak the nature of our problems. The illness is represented in a physical form by the symptoms, but it is not the real illness. The actual source of the difficulty is how you feel about yourself.

It is well documented that one of the triggers of an eating disorder is a desire to change one's body shape. You may be dismayed and distressed by the way you look, your body image and shape. This distress then leads you to engage in maladaptive behaviour around food and eating that ultimately enables you to change the way you look and your body shape and weight.

However, there is another side to the eating disorder, as often people may engage in eating disorder behaviours as a way of managing difficult feelings. More often than not you will be unaware that you are using your eating disorder symptoms to alleviate distress about how you feel. You may be aware that you are trying to change your body shape through your eating disorder symptoms, but you may be less aware that you are also using the symptoms as a way of changing/managing feelings. For example, you may engage in food restriction to dull or numb painful feelings, you may binge eat to improve your mood, or you may excessively exercise to distract yourself from feeling unworthy.

This lack of awareness of the illness as a way of regulating emotion leads to a disconnect between mind and body, which can perpetuate the struggle. There are several aspects of emotion regulation that you may struggle with.

You may find it harder to alter mood states, to change your own negative mood by replacing negative thoughts with positive ones, and as a result you may tend to struggle to control your behaviour when very distressed. This can often lead to the development of irrational and impulsive behaviours. You may also struggle to make sense of your feelings. This may leave you feeling negative about yourself when you feel upset, and you struggle to validate your own emotional experience of the world.

You may not always understand why you behave this way around food. It is therefore the role of therapy to explore these links through conversations and discussion about symptoms, meaning and emotion. It is the role of the therapist to enable and empower you to open up and engage with your emotional experience of the world, to feel the positive change that this can bring, and contrast that with your rigid, closed, distressed and cut-off experience that often leads to the harbouring of distressing eating disorder thoughts and behaviours.

From an external perspective, it may look like you are doing well – you may even feel a degree of pleasure with your success, but on the inside feel that you are not meeting the expectations that you set for yourself. Not being or feeling good enough is the constant source of doubt preoccupying your mind.

Central to the idea of not being good enough is the fear of just being an ordinary person, who has not accomplished anything extraordinary in their life. Controlling food and a sense of hunger can feel like an achievement and creates a sense of security. Behaviours such as calorie counting, food restriction, excessive exercise, binge eating and purging are used to relieve anxieties and regulate emotions.

Initially you may find it difficult to reflect on your history, thinking that once the present becomes the past there is no value in recalling it, as regardless of the turn of events, nothing can be done to alter things. This is a very linear perspective. Obviously you cannot change the past and the pain you have experienced. However, the past continuously influences and determines your present choices and actions. Sometimes it can have a detrimental influence without you realizing it; sometimes you can continually make choices in a repetitive way that are damaging to your existence. When you begin to improve your awareness of personal events, you gain an ownership of your life, and have an insight into the emotional needs hidden underneath your suffering. Within this, if you can take a more systemic position, you together with your therapist can retell the story, acknowledging needs and reducing a sense of guilt that can sometimes develop through assuming fault, blame and responsibility. This empowers you to learn from your story and give your experiences meaning, allowing you to change the outcome based on previous learning.

Some people have shared their experiences of looking back with us:

> 'I must have been a sad child. I felt out of place. I remember I was quiet. I did listen to everyone, but I could not talk much and say my opinion. I did play with some very carefully chosen friends, but I was mainly guided during the playing. I could not let myself go. Something was stopping me from the inside. Whatever I wanted to do had to be calm and gentle, in order not to make anyone upset or annoyed.'

When the patient shared this memory in therapy, they were aware of what they were doing, but not necessarily the thoughts and feelings that led them to behave in this way, and they weren't perhaps aware of their sophisticated ability to sense intuitively the needs of their parents and their own drive to respond to them. This effortful management of the feelings of others is defined as emotion work, a sometimes psychologically distressing process of caring for and protecting others.[6]

Another central element of attributing meaning is related to taking responsibility and learning to mediate our relationships with others. The enigma of the eating disorder symptoms can be better understood by exploring the conflict between independence from and dependence on others and by finding mediation between our own individual and social needs. We grow up, in fact, by being pushed and pulled by two important drives: one leading us to affirm our autonomy and ourselves, the other encouraging us to reinforce our social identity. An eating disorder could express the person's difficulty regulating and finding a balance between a sense of belonging to our social context and the need for independence.[7]

In this way the eating disorder becomes a driving force that dictates life, as suddenly everything starts to revolve around it. It sets strict rules that must be adhered to, otherwise the sense of guilt is overwhelming and intolerable.

You may often feel that your eating disorder is your 'safe place', your sanctuary. To others, this concept seems bizarre and distorted. How can something that causes so much distress be of any value? Therein lies the paradox of an eating disorder, which leaves parents and carers with a strong sense of disempowerment.

Women more than men have always had to fight for their own independence, to avoid being considered as objects to

be used for productivity, reproduction and sexual posses-
sion. Eating disorders in fact mostly affect women. However,
they are becoming more common in men, as they also have
to follow cast-iron rules demanding from them constant
mental and physical strength and productivity. Expected
by society to become powerful and aggressive, boys reject
the idea of becoming adults.

The eating disorder can be an expression of that conflict.

*'I felt my life had always been controlled firstly by educa-
tion, then university, then work, then relationships, then
parenthood. I needed to be good at all these things to be
a good person. I also felt I had to look a certain way, and
this was reinforced sometimes by family and sometimes by
social situations!'*

The essential fight for this person was against a controlling and oppressive social and moral code. The fear of
depending on relationships and social contexts that do not
acknowledge the uniqueness of the person expresses itself
as a strong and immovable opposition, as the idea of being
self-sufficient without needing any type of relationship with
the world, food included.

Within an eating disorder, controlling and restricting
food also controls the needs of the physical body. Controlling food equates to controlling and protecting your
identity. However, the eating disorder code is as strong and
oppressive as the social code against which you try to push.
Therefore, the tyranny of the illness leads to isolation, and
every time you allow yourself to have some food, extreme
guilt is experienced. The sense of guilt then reinforces the
eating disorder punitive cycle.

The treatment of an eating disorder always has to consider both physical and psychological levels. From a physical point of view, a medical and nutritional intervention has to preserve and improve health. From a psychological point of view, the clinician needs to help you to develop your own self and identity in a helpful and constructive way, not through the eating disorder symptoms. This requires going through the separation process from parental figures, and from certain social values experienced as demanding, controlling and punitive. An authentic exploration to stimulate your curiosity, with an emphasis on a not-knowing stance, would allow you to get closer to a truer sense of yourself.

Your emotional needs are important

When working with people with eating disorders we often hear how compliant they are. Parents are often shocked by their young person's level of determination not to eat, as troubling, non-compliant behaviour has never really been an issue in the past. The same is true of adults with eating disorders. These people are often described very positively by family and carers, as kind and thoughtful and always thinking of others, and thus these difficulties seem very out of character and so different from how people experience them more generally.

Under normal circumstances, personality traits such as selflessness and thoughtfulness are highly valued and well thought of. However, in eating disorders these personality traits can be so ingrained that you can put other people's needs before your own to the extent that you compromise your own needs and endure a degree of emotional pain and suffering because of this. The constant and pervasive prioritizing of other people's needs above your own leads to a diminished sense of self to the point where you do not even know what your preferences are even if you were able to follow them.

This type of behaviour is often described as 'people pleasing', but in many ways this term does not really describe the true damage that can be done by constantly devaluing your own needs to meet those of others. This pattern of behaviour can leave you feeling unable to express your needs and preferences and unable to hold boundaries in your own life. Often when you struggle to stick with a decision that you have made because of the impact of someone else's views, you can be left with negative, angry feelings.

If you think for a minute to a time in your own life when you experienced a degree of social pressure to do something that you didn't want to, you may also remember that following that experience you also felt a degree of resentment. However, the fear of disapproval from others is so great that the resentment is easier to bear. We may all be able to relate to that experience, but now try to imagine that every choice or decision that you make in your life is like this – this is what life can be like when you have an eating disorder. Over time these negative feelings that are not acknowledged or owned by the person turn into something very destructive, and the eating disorder symptoms can be a way of managing these feelings. This may not be at all obvious to the person with the eating disorder or those around them, but this type of pattern can often be identified through therapeutic work.

Families and carers ask us how this can be. The answers aren't obvious or easy to find. Many of you, since you were very little, will have been subjected to a strong demand for achievement; you have a busy schedule full of school and recreational activities where you can learn and develop your skills. From a parental and educational perspective, it is widely believed and accepted that this will produce a sense of accomplishment that will heighten your self-esteem. A strong sense of self is something that is highly valued and sought after. You do well and are successful and brilliant. Very soon, though, a sense of duty and discipline takes the place of the joy of playing. You do things without having had the chance to explore what you like. You develop a social role detached from a sense of self. You are excellent at whatever you do, but you feel empty. Within the external world around you, observers see a strong-willed person, full of commitment and determination.

However, internally you feel empty and angry for suppressing your needs. Your behaviours have a double meaning. They say 'yes' to others, and 'no' to yourself. The eating disorder symptoms are your way of being able to keep saying yes to others. In fact, you continue showing your dedication to others, but by refusing and controlling food, you start refusing and controlling the relationship with them. By saying 'no' to food, you say 'no' to what they think were their requests, their expectations. This can be a very painful journey because it means you have to try and assert yourself, and at the same time deny your need for enjoyment and comfort. Eating disorder symptoms manifest when you are not able to affirm your own needs and stand up for them. The reality of situations becomes categorical, such as devotion versus betrayal; sense of duty versus sense of guilt; discipline versus laziness; and isolation versus dependency. What is so often missing in your life is the fluidity within any form of relationships, the idea of self-achievement through enjoyment and pleasure, not only through an imposed and strict discipline. The sense of guilt is what prevents you from enjoying yourself and listening to your own needs. Everything achieved is a way of proving to others that you are worthy. However, others' approval is not an appropriate means to improve self-esteem.

In these moments, you may have feelings develop that can overwhelm you as the sense of grandiosity fails as soon as you are not on top, or whenever you suddenly get the feeling you have failed to live up to some ideal image or have not measured up to some standard. Then you are plagued by anxiety or deep feelings of guilt and shame.[8] When the place of playing is disrupted by the drive of discipline and achievement, access to the world of emotions and imagination becomes blocked.

Prioritizing others' needs means that your own needs will be suppressed or dismissed. This will lead you to do only what you feel is expected of you by others, but not what is wanted by your true self. A false sense of self develops, and it becomes harder to differentiate this from your true self. You find it harder to listen to and express your own needs. An eating disorder allows you to represent your ideal of not having any needs at all and being completely self-sufficient.

The development of eating disorder symptoms allows you to not respond to your sense of hunger, be it physical or emotional. You don't want to feel hunger, you don't want to feel happy or sad. You feel you are not entitled to those feelings. You feel obliged, a sense of duty to be cheerful for someone else, to suppress your own distress to accommodate the needs of others. You may feel oppressed by a sense of guilt for a considerable part of your life. You feel you have to meet other people's expectations and you constantly have to prove your sense of worth through enduring tasks dutifully.

This feeling can be rooted in the earliest period of life, and it cannot be simply solved or softened by intellectual arguments and a rational insight. It can only be transformed, slowly, by accessing the emotional internal world, with the help of a therapeutic relationship, where you and the therapist put into play your own selves with a reciprocal respect and understanding.

Paradoxically, the eating disorder becomes a protection from the demands of life and relationships. Solving the enigma of this intricate symptom is the only way to develop a more authentic identity. Once the unhelpful pattern has been identified, ways of making changes can be discussed. In many ways this work is related to the understanding of positive assertiveness. Interestingly, when we begin these discussions, patients often view assertiveness as something that feels aggressive and not something to be desired. However, through the process of the work, this can be explored so that assertiveness and the skills that accompany it can be seen as positive skills to be practised and valued. It is often easier to start practising these skills with people you are comfortable with, in situations that are familiar. We sometimes suggest asserting a choice about what movie to watch or which direction to go on a walk; prior to this the response of the person with the eating disorder would have been 'I don't mind' or 'I don't have a preference'.

'During some of my therapy session we started to talk about how good I was at making decisions. I was quite surprised to realize that this was something I really struggled with.

At first, I couldn't see the relevance of this to my eating difficulties. But as we talked more and I realized that my struggle with decisions was related to my need to meet everyone else's need before my own, I could see how that left me feeling. It was really helpful to know this about myself.'

'At first when my therapist told me to choose the film that we were going to watch as a family I thought it was odd. I really believed that I didn't mind what we watched, but once I was brave enough to share my view and we watched the film I chose then I realized how nice that felt – for my view to be positively received and for my needs to be met in that tiny moment.'

Alongside the development of assertiveness, the therapeutic process also needs to explore how to deal with disapproval, because once you start to express your own view, eventually you will come across some level of disapproval or criticism. People who have eating disorders struggle to manage the disapproval of others, so the work also needs to focus on how to manage your own feelings about what other people may be thinking about you, so that you can manage criticism without it impacting on your own sense of self-worth.

Therapy work needs to focus on personal resilience to help tolerate and manage criticism even when it is not delivered in a kind and constructive way. Part of this work is learning how to let go of other people's values, and to reflect on your own purpose and values. You are not simply here to please others and to be approved of by others. You are an individual with your own thoughts, feelings and beliefs, all of which are valuable and important, and you have a contribution to be made.

The pitfalls of comparison

When talking about the themes that generally come up in therapy for eating disorders, we need to spend some time thinking about the role of comparison within our lives. In many ways, it is impossible not to encounter some form of comparison when growing up. From the moment that we are born we are monitored, and our progress is charted to ensure that our development and growth are 'typical' compared to others of a similar age. When we slip or fall off from that developmental trajectory there can be further interventions to ensure that we get back on track. This kind of monitoring is very helpful, as it ensures that children and young people stay safe and well and have the best environment to optimize their development and growth, but it also does mean comparison from an early age. When we are young, we are unaware of this process, our parents and carers carrying the burden and responsibility for our growth and development. However, as we grow up, this responsibility becomes our own, and we begin to look to others for our social validation.

During adolescence, this type of social comparison is normal and to some degree needed to ensure that we can develop a sense of independence away from our main care-givers (normally our parents and carers). This is in fact the main job to be undertaken in adolescence, and ensures that the development of identity and individuation can take place. However, on occasions the process of social comparison can become unhelpful, and can lead to the development of negative behaviours and patterns that impact on self-worth. This can be the case in eating disorders, as social comparison can serve as a tool to berate yourself and confirm how inadequate you feel. It can take on such a high value that you feel lost and empty. In this sense, it does not contribute to a sense of belonging to a group or community; on the contrary, it creates feelings of not being good enough, feelings of inadequacy that may result in loneliness and increase vulnerability and isolation.

> 'I used to continually compare myself to my friends. If one of my friends happened to do better than me on a test, the feelings of inadequacy it left me with were so strong in the end I just found it easier not to be around friends at these times. This made me feel like a really bad person, as really, I should have just been happy for my friends, but my own feelings were so strong I just couldn't.'

The young person who shared this was not only negatively affected by the experience of social comparison, but then also felt the weight of guilt because they could not feel happy for their friends when they did well or were successful. It is important to remember that this person was not jealous or unkind. They were happy that their friend had done well, but their feelings about their own performance created such pain that they couldn't engage in that, and their main focus was their inadequacy.

This may be a common experience for many of you. Social comparison creates feelings of inadequacy that are so strong that isolating from friendship groups becomes an easier option, thus reinforcing the isolation that an eating disorder can bring. This creates a social distance that means the eating disorder becomes a safe place, as the eating disorder allows you to control your environment to such a degree that you do not have to encounter or manage such difficult feelings.

When trying to challenge the negative thoughts about self-worth that social comparison can create, we normally focus on trying to balance the thoughts by holding onto the idea that, often, we are only comparing ourselves to the best bits of other people rather than the whole of them, and this in itself is very unhelpful. We focus on trying to think of people as a whole, and yes, they may excel in one area on one instance, but there will be setbacks that everyone has to deal with. There is no one who doesn't struggle at some point – to imagine that there is this perfect person is setting up an unrealistic ideal of fantasy. Perhaps it is nice to have a fantasy like that, but of course it can only be a fantasy as that perfect person with that perfect life really doesn't exist.

The example above was linked to academic achievement, but social comparison can be about anything; often it is about body image, achievements and relationships. Comparisons can be made in almost everything we do and say. This process has only been intensified by some aspects of social media, and this at times can be very unhelpful. The fact that now there can be a constant stream of images that are meant to reflect perfection, whether it be the way a person should look or the way they should be living, means that it is very difficult to form your own views on different aspects of life, when there seems to be a code of conduct represented in the form of images bombarding us all the time. It is important that as individuals managing this we are able to set a boundary around social media and limit the impact it has on our lives and how it shapes our values and attitudes.

Perfectionism

Eating disorders originate from extremes of personality such as extreme reluctance to express emotion, slow adaptability to change, conformity, excessive rumination and perfectionism. All these aspects make adaptations to pubertal challenges difficult. Patients tend to avoid bringing hardship and suffering by turning to the eating disorder to silence needs, yearnings and emotional tensions they may fear. Perhaps more importantly, eating disorders can be used to shield the self from underlying fears that loved ones will fail to appreciate the inner struggle of unmet needs or emotions, thereby protecting the self from being exposed to potentially unbearable disappointments. Eating disorders therefore become a subconscious solution to facing pubertal challenges and life demands.[9] Performance becomes more important than internal needs. Perfectionism is a term that we often hear when working in the field of eating disorders.[10] People with eating disorders are often described as having very high standards, with perfectionist traits. This may be familiar to you; it is often related to a great fear of not being good enough and having to do better. This is often implicated in the onset and maintenance of eating disorders, anxiety disorders and depression. But what does perfectionism really look like in an eating disorder, and why is it so important to understand what drives this personality trait and how it relates to a person's internal world?

'I was very protected and looked after as a child. Since very little, as soon as I was finding it difficult to do something, from completing a drawing to fixing a toy, I was immediately rescued by my parents, also through the help of my

brother, five years older than me. Louis! Help your sister! She is not able to do this or that! Louis was very patient and caring towards me, he rarely showed his frustration at having to assist his little sister all the time for no real specific reason. What, I guess, I learnt from this is that I was not allowed to make mistakes or fail. You do something right, or you do not do it at all, because otherwise you will be a burden for someone else who has to rescue you. I always did what was expected.'

When a person is always praised for their diligence and self-containment, there is a level of expectation set, and they feel obliged to meet it. The person devotes time and energy trying to outguess others and to do what they think is expected of them.

You may not always strive to create an image of yourself as perfect – you are not narcissistic in that sense – instead you seek to perform so that you are accepted, so you will fit in and feel at ease. Your expectations for yourself often become higher; grades need to be better. There is no pleasurable sense of achievement; rather, you rarely feel good enough. There is no positive emotional experience either, but rather a depression or anxiety about failing to measure up to your own impossible standards. You are not always aware of this, but may describe an immense sense of tiredness, and lack of enjoyment or pleasure. Also, you are not able to work out what would make you feel better: anything related to self-nurture does not feel productive or pleasurable, rather it feels weak and self-indulgent. The idea of personal pleasure becomes linked with guilt. These feelings are relentless, profound and persistent, making you feel trapped. You find it difficult to sort out what is important or to maintain a sense of proportion. A small detail that has been missed may prevent you feeling any pleasure in a job otherwise well done. You are constantly on the alert for what is wrong and seldom focus on what is right. Playful experiences are not valued, curiosity about the world is not engaged in. Experiences have to be purposeful, like a goal that can be measured, a task that can be achieved. Activities cannot be undertaken for enjoyment alone.

It is difficult to understand what contributes to the development of a perfectionist stance. Sometimes insecurity can intensify the need for acceptance. In eating disorders social acceptance can be more highly valued than self-acceptance, and thus the pattern begins where the need for approval from others becomes greater than the need for self-acceptance. Perfectionism becomes an obsession, and the fear of not being good enough spurs you on to renewed efforts. A relentless and punitive pursuit of perfection becomes a set of rules that you must live by to escape any guilt that is created if you deviate from this pathway. Once the drive for perfection was seen as external, coming from other people, but over time the drive becomes internalized. It is no longer others driving your desire for perfection – you now demand it of yourself. People with eating disorders are often self-critical and lacking in any capacity to self-nurture or offer self-compassion.

Perfectionism is motivated, therefore, both by an effort to create a better sense of self or self-image and to obtain certain responses from other people. Your effort to turn in a perfect performance is a bid for approval, attention or acceptance, but it is only one ploy in an all-out campaign. Others are compliance and conformity. Personal interests or desires are pushed aside if they conflict with the wishes of others. The need to please others, no matter what the cost, is the compelling motive. As a consequence, personal emotional growth is stunted.

In an effort to please others, you control and conceal hostility and aggression. In presenting yourself as 'good' or 'nice', you often struggle to present an authentic picture of yourself; you are presenting a false self, and the awareness of this represents a sense of betrayal, so you are unable to accept praise. Perfectionism is related to the ideal of the self, and failure to measure up may result in a sense of shame.

It is at times very painful for you to acknowledge these patterns in your life. Over time you may sometimes be able to make the link between your perfectionist standards, your upbringing and the personality of your parents. You may become angry with others who you sometimes feel take advantage of your devotion. However, you also have to accept that you are promoting and enabling this model, unable to place respectful boundaries in relationships.

Perfectionism is not just a personality trait; it is anchored to Western society. The social values of individualism, efficiency and competition that trap people in a cage of sense of duty, power and achievements are spread across whole Western societies. Therefore, when we look at the family dynamics, we should always put them into the broader historical and social context. There is no one to blame, neither parents nor genetics. However, we should think more critically about the social values and principles passed onto us. Children are by definition the most vulnerable category of our society. They are completely dependent on adults, and they will do whatever it takes to respond to their demands, needs and expectations in order to feel loved, accepted and safe.[11]

The constant pursuit of perfectionist values often

detaches a person from the real meaning of emotion. Every task or process becomes about the pursuit of being perfect, and it becomes much harder to connect to an internal world where emotion can be unpredictable and unsafe. As a way of coping, an individual may isolate, disconnecting from their own internal world and pursuing and valuing only what is perfect. Initially this can be seen in an eating disorder as the relentless pursuit of thinness, coupled with a high anxiety around body shape and body weight.

Over time, the quest for perfection and the suppression of any form of emotion become all-consuming, to the degree that the sense of self is lost. For many this happens at adolescence. The developmental phase of adolescence is key in terms of identity formation, and where there is suppression of emotion and rigid thinking there is also an inability to develop different dimensions of personality that form the identity.

For example, John in therapy described feeling unable to move from the position of being the pillar for the family. As a result, he was not able to undertake the important task of identity development. Instead, he had to maintain his usual position, smiling, steady and quiet, and continue to be the person that he felt his family needed despite his own emotional and developmental needs. There was no way to set a boundary or to assert his own needs within this without feeling the weight of guilt for abandoning the family and letting people down.

For many people with eating disorders, the need for identity, which is a vital drive in the self-development process, takes another route: self-destruction disguised as self-improvement. What leads to perfectionism are qualities such as a strong sense of morality, responsibility and sensitivity to other people's social needs. People with these qualities always tend to think about how they can improve themselves, and the world around them. They also feel responsible for other people's well-being, and they try to protect them at all costs. A crucial part of the therapy process is to help people to recognize their qualities behind the symptomatic behaviours, so that they can redefine their sense of worth. We also help them see that the quest for perfectionism is a trap that they can get caught in. However, being focused on being perfect in every sense can stop people making any progress at all, and therefore it becomes paralysing and debilitating. Perfectionism is not the pathway to success on any level; it is more the pathway to unhappiness. It is important to help a person make these links in therapy.

Chapter 7

When Does Therapy End?

This final part of our book focuses on the idea of moving away from the eating disorder, and from the therapy process, towards a more enjoyable life. For many of you reading this, you may be thinking that the ending is easy to determine – it is when the situation has improved – and yes, of course, this is very important. However, the ending process is so much more than that. The theme of ending was also very evident in the letters that were written to us, and we wanted to dedicate a chapter of the book to this theme, alongside our own thoughts about the importance and value placed on endings. We will first discuss the notion of 'bumps in the road', the idea of slips that can create anxiety and distress and how these bumps can sometimes be forerunners to the actual ending. What ending, in all its different forms, represents, and what that can look like to different people, will also be discussed. Finally, we want to talk about what we take with us when the work ends. This refers to the many ways that you can carry the learning with you on your onward journey. It is these things that will see you through the other challenges that living a full and purposeful life will bring you. We hope that the recovery process has enabled you to recognize the desire within you to live that full and purposeful life.

Before ending

Bumps in the road

Whilst this chapter is dedicated to the idea of ending therapy work, it is important to also talk about the 'pre-ending stage', as sometimes it is discussion relating to ending therapy that can lead to a relapse. In this chapter we will refer to this as 'bumps in the road'. These 'bumps in the road' represent the anxiety that is sometimes created by the potential ending of support.

> 'I was doing well with my treatment and then my therapist started to talk about ending the sessions. This made me feel upset, as whilst I knew that things were going well, I did not feel better. I felt the thoughts were getting louder again and the behaviours slipped back in.'

So we know by now that eating disorders develop over time, and that they can be long-lasting disorders that have severe physical and emotional consequences. We have also established that accessing treatment is a helpful way to work through these issues. Managing food and potential triggers is an important part of treatment, but understanding and dealing with the emotional fractures and blockages can also help to maintain the healthy eating behaviours that represent recovery. In this chapter we want to talk to you about 'relapse prevention'. Relapse prevention is the idea that if you can anticipate where the difficulties may be in your recovery you can prepare for them, thus reducing their impact or helping you to manage them in a safe way. This is a very sensible approach for all areas of life, regardless of what the emotional difficulties or illness may be.

> 'The more I learnt about my eating disorder and the areas that I found difficult to manage, the easier it was for me to anticipate where I might have more stress and when I was more vulnerable. At the same time, the more I learnt about what helped me in those moments and what I found empowering, the more confident I felt about managing. These two things together helped me to manage my set-backs as they came and went.'

The warning signs related to slipping back into eating disorder behaviours can be varied and different for each individual. For some it will involve food-related behaviours such as increasing the number of times you weigh yourself, skipping meals, increasing exercise, or eating certain trigger foods. For others it may not be related to food or exercise at all, but may be more subtle, for example struggling to look in the mirror, avoiding social gatherings, or simply wanting to spend more time alone as that may feel more comforting and less exposed. It can be all of these things and none of these things as well. It is also important to note that although it can be the re-emergence of old behaviours that were associated clearly with the eating disorder, it can also be the development of new behaviours that were not part of the illness previously. These new behaviours may be driven by preoccupations with food and exercise, but they can catch you unaware as they may not be things that are associated with the eating disorder. This can also be very difficult for loved ones trying to support you, as they may not always recognize problem behaviours if they are new. This is not an easy task, and many loved ones also feel nervous about mentioning behaviours they are worried about for fear of making the situation worse. They may be reminded of a far more difficult time, but it is important for them to pay attention to those feelings as opportunities that are well placed and valid. For you, though, it is important to be brave and honest, to open up to people around you and ask for help, as it may be that a little more support is needed at this stage. For loved ones observing these changes the advice is basically the same: it is important to be brave and firm with your loved one, and talk them through what you are seeing and how you are making sense of it. It is better to be open as soon as possible about this so help can be accessed if needed.

The most important key message to remember is to get help when needed. There is no shame in relapse, it certainly does not mean failure: on the contrary, it means that as an individual you are resourceful and insightful enough to know that at this stage in the journey, for whatever reason, more support is needed. That being said, it is still very difficult to revisit a stage of recovery that you felt was over. The feeling of slipping back is very powerful, and it can be very scary to think you may have to work through things again. At this stage it can be helpful to revisit what motivated you to recover in the first place. What value did you place on recovery? How did this fit with your bigger life plans? How do you begin to re-engage with those ideas?

It might also be helpful to think what is happening in your life at the moment. Are you going through any new or challenging situations or experiencing specific emotions that might be confusing, and you are relying on the eating disorder behaviours because they bring a sense of familiarity? In situations like these, it could be helpful to see the eating disorder behaviours as signals that are there to tell you to slow down for a moment and check in with yourself whether there are any unmet needs. The more you become comfortable with checking in with yourself and exploring your emotions and thoughts, the less the eating disorder symptoms will resurface.

It is very important for all involved to be compassionate and understanding in spite of the fear that relapse may create within you. Respect, honesty and trust are key at this stage. Remembering to ask for help is a positive thing that suggests there is good self-awareness about what is needed at this stage.

Managing setbacks

Most of you with eating disorders will experience some form of relapse at some point on your journey. The severity of the setback will be determined by the factors discussed above, but it is a very normal phase of getting better and working towards ending therapy. It is important that you have realistic expectations about what relapse is and what can be learnt from it, as so much can be taken from these experiences.

Relapse can also be a very difficult time for families and carers. Family members and carers may have just started to feel secure with some of the changes that have occurred.

They have been wanting this stage of recovery for so long, and trusting it can be difficult. They may have finally got to that point, and for whatever reason it begins to slip. The fear and anxiety that this can create is very real and significant. It is very easy and understandable to panic and be drawn back to really difficult times, with traumatic memories of just how hard it all was in the beginning, of the impact it had on themselves, the person with the eating disorder, and the whole family. The feeling of simply not being able to go back to that position becomes all-consuming and very frightening.

For parents and carers reading this book, remember that it can feel just like that for the people with the eating disorder as well. However, you are not powerless in this situation – it is not as it was. It is important to remember that recovery is not always a consistent experience. There will be good and bad days, and whilst we are always told to focus on consistency, it is not something that is easily achieved. If you feel that the recovery process is very inconsistent, try to refocus on why these changes were needed, and break down some of the larger recovery tasks into small goals which may feel more achievable on difficult days.

If you are a loved one observing this process, have an open conversation with the person about what you notice. Share with them your thoughts in a way that is open and honest and demonstrates an open approach in terms of trying to understand their responses, which may at times create anxiety within you. It is important that everyone in the process acknowledges that it is not possible every day to do everything you can to recover, or to do everything you can to support recovery.

If on some days only small things can be done, then that can be enough. This should be viewed as positive, as in these moments you are setting out the building blocks for more good habits to grow and develop, and this is very helpful and encouraging. It is also important not to be too hard on yourself when you are struggling on the bad days – this is relevant to the person with the eating disorder and their parent or carer. It is the easiest thing in the world to tell someone not to be too hard on themselves, but applying this to ourselves can be much harder.

When you have been struggling with eating disorder thoughts and behaviours, telling yourself to stop isn't easy, but we can begin to notice our thought processes more and respond in a way that gives these thoughts less power. Our responses can then create distance from the thoughts, and it becomes easier to resist them.

In many ways this demonstrates the idea of self-compassion very neatly. It allows a degree of self-respect and values the idea of self-compassion, rather than us struggling to hold in mind the idea of anything other than being pitiful or struggling.

Alongside bad days there may also be days when nothing has gone right, when nothing has gone to plan, when it has been really difficult to hold in mind the idea of recovery. It is important to know that it is okay to have those days as well. On the days when nothing seems to have gone right, try to remember the basics of what helps us to stay balanced. Try to focus on achieving good sleep, or engaging in some aspects of the recovery routine, and finally draw on the value you place in the human connections you have around you. On a really bad day when nothing has gone right, the people who love you the most will help to get you through. This is important information for all of you.

We are all always human beings from the beginning to

the end, and it is our relationships that can see us through very dark moments. Remember to draw on them and try to resist the urge to isolate, as that can make things harder. Remember to focus on all the knowledge and strength that has been gained through the process, and take that with you into the next mini-battle with the disorder.

It is important to remind yourself that whilst it feels like you may be returning to the same situation, you are not. This time round you have more skills, knowledge and experience, and whilst the powerful feelings take you right back to that difficult place, the situation is different. *You* are now different; you operate in a different way, and that in itself will create a different response within you which can impact the situation differently. Feelings can be very powerful, they can trick us into thinking you are back where you started, but you rarely are; you are different from what you were as you cannot help but be changed by your experience.

Self-confidence and self-acceptance

When therapy has been a positive experience there is so much that you and the therapist can take from the work. Ideally, through the process, there will have been times when the therapy has extended outside of the session and has been generalized to other aspects of life. This is therapy when it works well. When therapy ends well there should be things that you leave with that accompany you forever on your onward journey. These may be part of conversations that you hadn't understood in the moment, but with reflection and other life experiences they click into place.

'Sometimes in therapy I did not see the relevance of all the

conversations. It was only maybe later when the therapy had ended, when certain situations reminded me of a conversation and something that felt valuable. It was almost like the purposefulness of this was a bit delayed, but it was really helpful when it clicked into place. It is really difficult to explain how that experience feels but it is almost like a little reminder of what you can take with you when the therapy work comes to an end, and it was comforting to know that this can happen.'

Ideally on ending you take with you a newfound sense of self-confidence and self-acceptance. These two concepts are often linked together but in many respects are quite different. The growth of self-confidence is always seen as a valuable thing. People who are described as self-confident are often seen as assertive and positive, willing to take on new challenges with a sense of self-belief. This is an important aspect to consider, as being self-confident and continuing to grow and develop within this is not about always living a comfortable, safe life. It is about personal growth and development, which sometimes means pushing yourself to new limits that may create fear. It is not about avoiding those situations.

Recovering from an eating disorder is about facing many different challenges. This can look like different things for different people. For some it may be about conquering the fear of eating out in restaurants, and not just staying with the safe restaurants where you know the menu and can order something you are used to, but pushing yourself to go to the restaurant where you are not sure of the meal content or how they cook the food. You push yourself to go as you want to experience something new that is not related to an eating disordered way of coping. This is a brave thing to do in terms of recovery, and quite often when tasks like this are achieved the confidence that can be built from them is really positive. Of course, there are so many situations that might be challenging for people recovering from an eating disorder – eating a meal out is just one of them. But the important point is that it is only by going where we feel the fear that we can then develop the self-confidence to progress on our journey. When we can tolerate the fear and allow ourselves to feel vulnerable, self-confidence grows from within us.

Another aspect of this is the ability to tolerate any failure that occurs. It would be unrealistic to assume that every time the fear is tolerated the outcome will be positive. Sometimes it may be difficult, and the vulnerable feelings will persist. It is important on these occasions that you are able to reflect on that, not see this as a failure, and not let it damage your self-confidence. It is important to accept that you are not defined in life by any aspect of life you fail at. Every failure or mistake can be a learning curve, where something valuable can be taken and applied to the next situation. To be able to take the learning away with you, you need the capacity to reflect. You need to move away from any shame you may feel from your failure and embrace it as an everyday aspect of learning that is as valuable as, perhaps even more valuable than, your successes. If you think back to times in your life when you experienced failures, you may appreciate over time that you learnt more from those instances than from situations that turned out well.

Self-acceptance is another important concept to draw on in therapy. Self-acceptance is sometimes presented as the idea that you are completely comfortable with yourself, that you accept where you are in life and as a result you are happy to sit in that position and feel settled. This in many ways does the idea of self-acceptance a disservice. It suggests that people who are more self-accepting may not be interested in further personal growth and development. They are content and satisfied where they are. However, self-acceptance is not really this at all. It is more the idea that if we are accepting of who we are and not battling against it we are more able to face the challenges that we encounter in a positive self-affirming way. So it is linked to the idea of self-awareness and self-reflection. Those people in life who have developed the capacity to reflect on their own situations are generally more aware of themselves, and once you have a greater sense of who you really are, you are in a better position to accept that and face the challenges that life can create with that knowledge in mind. In many instances the challenges may be difficult, but they are armed with the self-awareness and understanding of themselves that will help see them through.

A positive therapy experience would include reflective conversations to support you to develop a greater sense of self-awareness to help you in your life. You leave therapy with a compassionate and realistic appraisal of who you really are, which equips you with the skills and knowledge to manage the tough bits of life. In many ways this idea could not be further from the idea of self-acceptance that is often conveyed in the media. It is an important difference, and in terms of ongoing recovery it is very important to have a realistic understanding of what the challenges are going to be and where there will be struggles. You can then have a realistic understanding of when you can manage and when you may need support. This can be an ongoing conversation with those around you, with openness and transparency from the start. The more open you can be about the potential pitfalls, the more likely you are to overcome them positively. Hiding away from life challenges suggests that there are still things about the illness that create shame in you and you feel the need to hide. Ideally the process of therapy will have challenged this idea and you will be in a better place to share this with those around you so you can access the support as you need it.

Finding purpose and meaning

As we have already mentioned, when you come to therapy seeking support with an eating disorder you often want to be free of the eating disorder thoughts and feelings that have kept you locked into a prison of behaviours that have deeply affected your life experiences. These thoughts, feelings and behaviours will have shaped attitudes that you have towards your relationship with food and your body. These aspects of the eating disorder may have been the first thing that you felt and may well have been the first change that family members/carers and partners noticed in you. However, over time the patterns of behaviour and thinking related to the eating disorder will have had a much bigger impact on your life. They may have affected choices you have made and created difficulties within your interpersonal relationships. The rigidity of the patterns may have limited life experiences to a degree where you became unhappy and anxious even when engaging in activities related to normal functioning. The eating disorder may have damaged your life to such an extent that your functioning became very limited and, even more concerning, you became happy with this limited existence.

Through the process of recovery and ongoing support from therapy and those around you, you may now have managed to find your way back to your life, and are facing the question of how to move on from that phase in your life and seek out other ways to give it meaning and purpose and to experience happiness.

The idea of 'just wanting to be happy' is a common one. Young people often share with us in therapy that they 'just want to be happy'. When parents are asked about their hopes for their children, they often start by saying, 'We just want them to be happy.' This sets up the idea that long-lasting happiness is something that should be easy to achieve, but realistically, no one is happy all of the time. Given that we are emotional beings that experience a range of emotions on a day-to-day basis, it is unrealistic to think that through the process of life we won't experience a range of emotions including sadness, anger and guilt. The idea of happiness being a constant state where these emotions do not exist is unrealistic and unhelpful. Sometimes we will not feel happy, sometimes we will feel sad, sometimes we will feel over-whelmed; this is because we are human beings who make human connections and as a result feel a range of emotions. To be constantly happy would mean we would never feel sadness when we lose someone, which would inevitably mean we would never experience the strength of feeling and human connection that loss can create. When we reshape it like this, it is easy to understand that when you live a full and meaningful life you will encounter a range of emotions. Ideally when you have recovered from your eating disorder you can engage in these emotions and understand what they create within you and have the skills and understanding to tolerate the fear and work through the difficulties and pleasures that a full and meaningful life will bring to you.

Saying farewell to the eating disorder?

Alongside the notion of relapse prevention is the idea of saying farewell to the eating disorder. Many family members and carers will not only be ready to say farewell, but will also want to say a firm, solid goodbye. They will want to say that the eating disorder is not welcome back, such was the impact the illness had on the family and family life. For you the concept of farewell may not be so straightforward. Regardless of the pain and suffering the eating disorder will have caused you and the people around you, it will also have served a purpose and held a value. The process of therapy will have hopefully unearthed much of this purpose, and also helped you to adjust and change certain behaviours to more healthier ways of responding and coping. However, there still may be a degree of sadness and loss that accompanies the ending stage. For some the eating disorder will have started as a safe place to hide and it may have felt like a good friend. For many it may have stayed at this level for a long time. For others it may have been more of an 'on/off' friend, sometimes feeling friendly and making the sufferer feel safe and secure, at other times feeling like a bully, making you feel lost and out of control.

Regardless of what the eating disorder represented, there was a relationship with it, and when a relationship of any kind draws to a close there can be a sense of loss and sometimes a sense of grief. It is important that you can understand this process. Sadness and grief are often linked together, but grief is much more than sadness: there is an intensity and yearning within it that is almost intolerable. Sometimes endings that are significant in our life can trigger a grief response even when that ending is not caused by death. The pain caused by grief can be emotional and physical, and it is not always possible to take the pain away. It is important that the pain is worked through to a better end, as otherwise the process can get stuck, and the grieving process can move from something that is natural to something more maladaptive.

When supporting any grief process that may be experienced as part of the ending process, it is important that the sadness and value of what has been lost can be acknowledged. As already mentioned, this is hard for family and carers to understand, as although the eating disorder will have held a value for you, to them it only appears to have brought pain and suffering. It is also important at the same time to acknowledge why the disorder and the symptoms are no longer needed: you now understand more about the dysfunction and the illness, and you do not need these patterns of behaviours to keep yourself safe any more as you have new ways of coping and new ways of being. This may be a therapeutic conversation or a conversation with a family member, but it is important that there is an expression of this somewhere in the process so it can be reflected on as a natural part of the process. Ideally the mind and body can move through this process at the same time, so physical symptoms of the eating disorder can be given up at the same time as emotional aspects of it. In this way the mind and body are in tune rather than at odds; many times through the disorder they will have been at odds with each other, causing an intolerable conflict. It is important through the process of recovery that this conflict can be moved past and resolved.

The structure provided by the recovery process can also help guide you through this. For example, you may find that you have more time on your hands, because some tasks previously took much longer due to ritualized behaviours and thought ruminations. As a result, you may need some help structuring that time so that you feel supported rather than lost. If this support can be offered constructively with a positive focus, then you will see how much more you can contribute to the world when engaged in positive patterns of behaviours and thoughts that enable you rather than trap you. It is at this point that you can really begin to feel free and ready from an emotional perspective to let go and say an empowered farewell.

Therapeutic endings

What do endings represent to us?

There are so many endings in life. Stage-of-life endings are often marked with some kind of ceremony or celebration, which does not acknowledge the sadness that some endings can create in our lives. In many ways this is because through life we tend to focus on the means of life, and we see everything we do simply as a way to get somewhere else. The risk of doing this is missing out on life altogether. Ideally, everything we do should be an end in and of itself, and be experienced fully, from the initial phase to its ending, independently from the goal that it allows us to achieve.

This is so true for people with eating disorders. In many

ways the focus on the means may be evident in many of your thought patterns and behaviours. Much of this book has focused on the task-orientated approach of people with eating disorders and the impossibly high standards that this can create, with the emphasis on what you can achieve rather than what you can experience through achieving it. When we treat the things we do as simply functional steps towards some future ends, function replaces meaning, and we transform our very selves into objects for the satisfaction of some future self. Therapy is the opposite of this: it has hopefully helped you to slow down life and stay in the moment, focusing on the emotion that the moment creates.

As we have already mentioned, many of you ask us for a timeframe for recovery. This is an understandable question. Another such question that arises at a different time but seems just as relevant and important is the question of when therapy can end. Ending therapy needs to be done carefully and elegantly; in many ways this is a core therapeutic skill for a therapist. Ending therapy well is just as important as the initial and middle phase, as ending well can create a new positive experience of things coming to an end. When we work with patients where there have been emotional regulation difficulties, there are often fractures in relationships that have shaped these difficulties. It is important that the ending of therapy is not fractured, that it is considered, that it is timely, and that it is a joint decision.

When and how to end therapy

When the therapeutic work reaches a certain stage, it is important that discussions about ending therapy take place within a safe and emotionally containing framework.

Bringing therapy to a close elegantly, carefully and kindly is very important. It's certainly not about moving you on at the first sign of improvement; rather it is about open conversations about why you ventured into therapy initially and whether your thoughts and feelings regarding this have been explored and your needs have been met. It is about setting clear guidelines and helping you to be emotionally ready to consider that your therapeutic journey is ready to end.

Within the context of the therapeutic relationship, emotional needs such as attention and intimacy will have been met. These are basic emotional needs that are important to most of us, and thus when therapy begins to draw to a close there can be an anxiety or fear about how this can be created elsewhere. This process will have been very meaningful for you, and it is important that these needs can be met outside of the therapy space as this will allow you to be able to move away from any feelings of dependency on the therapist. Sometimes therapists are aware that they may be the patient's only source of intimacy and attention. Encouraging people to seek out other relationships within their lives to meet these needs should be part of the work, otherwise people cannot be expected to want to end the therapy. In many ways our role as therapists is to help you with specific difficulties, but not to meet your basic needs on an ongoing basis.

As therapists, another important aspect of ending the therapy work is to revisit the initial phase of therapy and reflect on your aims and objectives in terms of your hopes about what therapy could be. This discussion will have formed the initial phase and be integrated in the process of the work. It will have been different things for different people, but everyone entering into the therapeutic relationship will have had some expectations, and these expectations will have been discussed. It is important to revisit these and think with you how much of the work has now been done and what remains left. The bit that is left may not need to be attended to within the therapy at this point, but it is important that you are aware that it is there. In many ways these expectations will not be new or surprising to you. They will have been there from the beginning, guiding the process.

'I started therapy as I wanted to be able to manage my eating disorder thoughts and change patterns of behaviour that were unhelpful to me. Together my therapist and I worked through this, and I managed to alter things. However, we also worked far more on my understanding of why I did these things in the first place, which has helped me not to slip back. I did not realize at the beginning that it was just as important to know this too.'

Staying in touch

Sometimes patients ask us if they can work towards an ending but perhaps also think about staying in touch. We feel that this can be a very lovely way for the therapeutic relationship to stay represented in the patient's life after the active phase of therapy has ended. Some do this and contact us now and again to book a review session, or a session to touch base and have a space to reflect on recent changes in their life that they would like to share with us in the context of the therapeutic relationship. Interestingly, many ask if they can contact us again and then never get in touch; we hope this group always feel they can if they feel the need. Sometimes knowing that you can is very helpful in holding a feeling that may be created by the ending.

'I really valued that my therapist told me I could keep in touch. I really believe that they meant it, and just knowing that I could do this really helped me to end my therapy sessions. I never did go back, but even now I know that I could and sometimes that thought is enough.'

This is a lovely way to work and as therapists we feel it is a positive, meaningful ending. This is our experience of managing endings, but you will discuss this with your own therapist and there may be other ways that you can stay in touch with your experience of recovery. Some people choose to remain in support groups where they can continue to share their experiences with others. Others choose to join eating disorder charities and become ambassadors or to share their experiences with other people struggling with eating disorders. These types of roles are often described as 'expert by experience' roles. People choosing to follow this pathway may offer talks to other people struggling on their journey, hoping to demonstrate that full recovery is possible. Sometimes experts by experience join quality networks for the development of eating disorder services and therapies. Sometimes people go on to write books and articles, sharing their journey in written words. As professionals working in the field, we both have the privilege of hearing experts by experience speak about their journey, and it is always such a humbling and insightful experience. These people add so much to the knowledge base, and we are always so grateful that they are willing to share.

Afterword

We would now like to share with you some final thoughts and say goodbye. We hope that you have found this book helpful, and we thank you for taking the time to read it.

There is still a question, related to us as therapists, that we feel is important to address. Very often at some point of the therapy process people ask us why we chose to become clinical psychologists and why we started working in eating disorders. In line with the idea of co-production and personalized treatment, we feel that it is important that therapists share some personal information about themselves that can help the therapeutic process, and reassure the person who is trusting us by asking for help and opening up to us that we too are involved in the process and will share in open dialogue in the therapeutic relationship. So we would like to tell you a bit about us here.

Lucia: When I think about the time I started specializing in eating disorders, this quote always comes immediately to my mind: 'The soul needs a place.' It was written by the Greek philosopher Plotinus (204/5–270 BCE) and was displayed at the entrance to the inpatient eating disorder service in Italy that I visited for the first time in 2006 for an internship. The service admits both adults and young people, and I recall my surprise at how little it resembled a hospital; it was warm and nurturing – almost homely – the atmosphere designed to provide an appropriate environment to foster recuperation and recovery, to allow inpatients the space to restore their physical and psychological health and to reconnect with themselves.

This experience came at the beginning of my clinical doctorate when I went out into the field for the first time. From the lectures, I understood that eating disorders lead the sufferer to reject, or abuse, one of the most elemental ingredients of our lives – food. I was also struck by how eating disorders affect the mind as well as the body, highlighting the importance of the circular connection between these two parts of our selves. A general lack of awareness of the illness, in conjunction with the degree of severity that this disorder can reach, was simultaneously both extremely upsetting and thought provoking from a psychological perspective. I felt it was very important to understand this in depth in order to understand more about us as human beings in general, as a relationship with food and the attempt to integrate the experience of our body and mind is something we all share.

Since I was very young, I felt that I wanted to become a clinical psychologist. I was always observing people around me, reflecting on the many questions I had about how and why they behaved or talked in a certain way. I was also always available to listen to them and they often came to confide in me. I did not know, though, in which field of clinical psychology I wanted to work. During the lectures on

eating disorders, a particular focus was given to perfectionism as a common personality trait shared by people with
eating disorders and considered a predisposing factor. The
question behind the weight and shape concerns and the
unhelpful eating behaviour/patterns is often, if not always,
'Am I good enough?', accompanied by the urge of having to
do more, achieve more, because you, as you are, don't feel
good enough. This aspect particularly resonated with me.
I could understand that behind that there was a quest for
identity, a desire to become a better person, to be and do
something meaningful. 'How can you understand me if you
never had an eating disorder?' patients often ask us. And I
tell them that although the symptomatic behaviours could
seem totally irrational to a person who never had an eating
disorder, I can grasp the meaning behind them because they
are not simply related to an illness but have to do with who
a person would like to become, the quality of their relationships, and the place they would like to have in the world.

In my first week in the service, I was given the opportunity to attend a philosophical group. I was deeply moved
by the conversations we had in the group. People were
approaching fundamental existential questions with a
strong determination, but they were also putting themselves at risk through those symptomatic behaviours.
Eating disorders are one of the few mental illnesses from
which, initially, a patient has little motivation to recover,
so the risk is even greater. At the same time, it became very
clear to me then that those psychological symptoms cannot be simply addressed from a behavioural point of view,
but they have to be interpreted and understood within the
personal, relational and socio-cultural context. They do not
indicate a deficit, that something is broken, but an attempt

to question the way people are living in certain situations and find a new path, a new meaning. The severity of the disorder is counterbalanced by a strong drive and need to learn more about themselves and life.

From that day, I continued working together with people with eating disorders and the many colleagues from different disciplines that form the multidisciplinary team. I always integrated the clinical work with research work, which is still at an early stage in this field. Despite the many years of experience, it remains a challenge. The results of the therapeutic work are sometimes seen years later when I receive letters from patients stating that at the time of treatment they did not allow themselves to openly acknowledge my words, but that they were nevertheless listening. Moments like this serve to reinforce my conviction that I am on the right path. I will not always be able to help and have the right words, but I know that I will continue to provide my contribution together with my colleagues, and to share my experience with and learn from the patients and the families I have the privilege to work with.

Sophie: From a very early age I was curious about people. I was always curious about where people were going, what motivated their decisions, why they made the choices they did. I enjoyed the fantasies I created in my head about them. I realized that studying psychology would provide a framework for understanding the way people work and help me to understand them. I was very fortunate to be encouraged to study and explore this passion by my family, who told me to be brave and bold in my choices. I enjoyed my undergraduate degree more than any other study I had undertaken and enjoyed learning about mental health. It was at that point I decided I wanted to pursue a clinical pathway. I think I had always liked being around children. I liked their innocence, their perspective on the world, and this has only intensified as I have grown older. Now I look at young people and I am so keen to hear what they think and what their perspectives are. The generation gap is fascinating to me as it creates different thinkers who are experiencing the world in a different way, and I can see that we can all learn so much from each other. In my final year placement of my clinical doctorate, I worked in an adolescent inpatient unit treating young people with eating disorders. The young people fascinated me and saddened me all at the same time. It was an interesting conflict in emotions for me to feel such passion and interest in an illness but at the same time to feel such fear and concern for the people suffering. On this placement I had such a talented, kind and compassionate supervisor who had the same passion as me. Together we developed a workbook of therapeutic tasks for engaging people with eating disorders in therapy. This became my first published therapy manual, and for that experience I am so grateful as it consolidated my interest in working within this area. Almost twenty years later, eating disorders still hold the same interest for me. I can now see more clearly that you need this type of interest to be able to have some longevity within this field. I still hold the same sadness, perhaps even more now as I have seen so much more suffering and pain. However, I also feel inspired by the people I meet, the strength of both the patients and the families to battle and recover as so many do. The psychologist in me is passionate about the ever-developing evidence base for treatment approaches. I not only believe in the evidence base as a psychologist, I also see its effectiveness in practice and this is the best part of being a scientist practitioner and clinical psychologist. At the same time, as psychologists, we are not magicians – we cannot solve all the problems, but we can share some of the knowledge and understanding we have to empower people to make the changes they need to improve their lives.

In terms of my day-to-day working life, I am fortunate to feel that I have done something purposeful and meaningful; this is indeed something to be valued, as I know it is not everyone's experience in life. It is this that drives me to continue to work in the way that I do, to help others experience something meaningful and valuable so that they too can go on to make a contribution and value the feeling that creates within them, be it through school life, working experiences or relationships. It is the human connection part of my job that really brings me this. To be able to experience that, psychological well-being is essential, and if I can be a tiny part of supporting that then I feel I am doing something worthwhile. I don't think I can ask for more than that.

The need to write this book together developed when we were still in the middle of the pandemic. It was driven by our desire to communicate with as many people as possible and foster a sense of belonging and connection with those whom we would not have a chance to meet but with whom we could share our values. The pandemic made us acknowledge more than ever our smallness as single individuals and reinforced the need to attempt to transcend this by imagining, when you wrote to us, that we were connecting with many people.

We had just completed our first book together on eating disorders for professionals, and we were receiving many emails and calls every day from patients, families and colleagues to ask whether we had availability for another person who was needing help with an eating disorder. We could witness the tremendous impact that the pandemic was having on the numbers of people with eating disorders, and both patients and colleagues felt at a loss and did not know where to start to address the problem. We felt therefore that we had to do something more than talking with one person at a time. In times of confusion, suffering and uncertainty, it is important to try to break things down, simplify what feels too complex and insurmountable, and connect with others.

Whilst we were passionate about writing this book, at times the task felt too big. How could we reliably capture the views of others and share them in a way that was helpful and constructive? It was important that we represented these views as authentically as possible, and that was a great responsibility. Even at the time of completing the writing process we were still being regularly contacted by concerned parents who were struggling to access the right care for their family member.

Given the strong need for a book of this nature, we want to be clear that we know that we have not been able to answer all your questions, and the answers provided are only partial, but we do hope that what we shared has provoked further questions and reflections so that our search for understanding and meaning can be explored further. The conversations can continue. And we are certain that they will continue – you might also have experienced that whenever you have addressed a problem, recovered from an illness or completed a meaningful project, you have reached a broader and more comprehensive understanding of yourself and the world, which will lead to yet more questions.

We would like to leave you with some final broad

concepts that we think it is important to share and continue to explore within and beyond the therapy room.

We often met patients who for years had not even contemplated the idea of therapy, but at the end of their therapy said that *everyone should go to therapy*, because they could see how every single person would benefit from exploring and taking care of their emotional well-being and psychological development. Going to therapy is not the only way to do that, but supporting the emotional understanding and development of people should definitely be one of our priorities as society. No financial, technological or intellectual progress will be constructive if not supported by emotional intelligence.

The other need represented by the phrase *everyone should go to therapy* is one of social connection consisting of open and honest conversations. We all know that the trend of competitive individualism needs to reverse to contain the damage it has caused at all levels. We need other people to exist and to give meaning to our life. This is scary at times, as it can make us feel dependent on others and therefore vulnerable. However, it is paramount that we work on finding a balance between our needs and the needs of the others, so that relationships can be fostered through reciprocity.

Some people realize that when they learn more about their eating disorder, they also better understand their or other people's anxiety or depressive symptoms. Often people come to us with a long list of diagnoses, which helps the professionals communicate quickly with each other, but is very overwhelming for the person, and it does not say really anything about them as a whole. It is important for all of us in our respective roles to move beyond the labels and observe and interrogate ourselves on the relational dynamics, the interconnections between thoughts, emotions and behaviours, and how we are interpreting our experience. Our being is dynamic and ever evolving. Alongside this, we should work together to move away from a disease-model approach when it comes to understanding our psychological condition.

An illness tends to narrow down our view of ourselves and life. Eating disorders specifically show very clearly the fractures that an illness creates between our mind and body, and also different parts of our life and in our relationships. We know by now that the treatment needs to be multidisciplinary, and care needs to involve not only the person affected but also their support system. A multidisciplinary or, even better, an interdisciplinary approach, where all the disciplines and persons involved collaborate with each other and integrate their point of view and knowledge, is always needed to recover, whatever meaning you attribute to your recovery at this point in time.

It is now time to say goodbye, but please do stay in touch, whether in a concrete way by writing to us with your comments and further questions, or in a more virtual way by supporting us by sharing the conversations we have had through this book, finding out more about eating disorders or being proactive towards your own or a loved one's recovery, and being curious and interested in the complexities of our minds even in times of suffering. These times are bridges to cross that can lead you to new unexpected positive developments.

References

Chapter 2

1   Smink, F. R., Van Hoeken, D., & Hoek, H. W. (2012). Epidemiology of eating disorders: Incidence, prevalence and mortality rates. *Current Psychiatry Reports, 14*(4), 406–414.

2   American Psychiatric Association (2013). *Diagnostic and Statistical Manual of Mental Disorders: DSM-5, fifth edition.* Washington, DC: American Psychiatric Association.

3   Fairburn, C. G., Cooper, Z., & Shafran, R. (2008). Enhanced Cognitive Behaviour Therapy for Eating Disorders: The Core Protocol. In C. G. Fairburn (ed.), *Cognitive Behaviour Therapy and Eating Disorders* (pp. 47–193). New York: Guilford Press.

4   Qian, J., Wu, Y., Liu, F., Zhu, Y., *et al.* (2022). An update on the prevalence of eating disorders in the general population: A systematic review and meta-analysis. *Eating and Weight Disorders, 27,* 415–428.

5   Haripersad, Y. V., Kannegiesser-Bailey, M., Morton, K., Skeldon, S., *et al.* (2021). Outbreak of anorexia nervosa admissions during the COVID-19 pandemic. *Archives of Disease in Childhood, 106*(3), e15.

Termorshuizen, J. D., Watson, H. J., Thornton, L. M., Borg, S., et al. (2020). Early impact of COVID-19 on individuals with self-reported eating disorders: A survey of ~1,000 individuals in the United States and the Netherlands. *International Journal of Eating Disorders, 53*(11), 1780–1790.

Touyz, S., Lacey, H., & Hay, P. (2020). Eating disorders in the time of COVID-19. *Journal of Eating Disorders, 8*(1), 1–3.

6 Lin, J. A., Hartman-Munick, S. M., Kells, M. R., Milliren, C. E., *et al.* (2021). The impact of the COVID-19 pandemic on the number of adolescents/young adults seeking eating disorder-related care. *Journal of Adolescent Health, 69*(4), 660–663.

7 Touyz, S., Lacey, H., & Hay, P. (2020). Eating disorders in the time of COVID-19. *Journal of Eating Disorders, 8*(1), 1–3.

Vyver, E., & Katzman, D. K. (2021). Anorexia nervosa: A paediatric health crisis during the COVID-19 pandemic. *Paediatrics and Child Health, 26*(5), 317–318.

Rodgers, R. F., Lombardo, C., Cerolini, S., Franko, D. L., *et al.* (2020). The impact of the COVID-19 pandemic on eating disorder risk and symptoms. *International Journal of Eating Disorders, 53*(7), 1166–1170.

8 Belkin, G., Appleton, S., & Langlois, K. (2021). Reimagining mental health systems post COVID-19. *Lancet Planetary Health, 5*(4), e181–e182.

9 Royal College of Psychiatrists (2022). *Medical Emergencies in Eating Disorders: Guidance on Recognition and Management.* www.rcpsych.ac.uk/docs/default-source/improving-care/better-mh-policy/college-reports/college-report-cr233-medical-emergencies-in-eating-disorders-(meed)-guidance.pdf (accessed on 19 December 2022).

10 Royal College of Psychiatrists (2012). *Junior MARSIPAN: Management of Really Sick Patients under 18 with Anorexia Nervosa.* www.otforeatingdisorders.co.uk/resources/Junior%20Marsipan%202012.pdf (accessed on 19 December 2022).

11 National Institute for Health and Care Excellence (NICE) (2017). *Eating Disorders: Recognition and Treatment* (NICE Guideline 143). www.nice.org.uk/guidance/ng69 (accessed on 19 December 2022).

12 Hay, P., Chinn, D., Forbes, D., Madden, S., *et al.* (2014). Royal Australian and New Zealand College of Psychiatrists Clinical Practice Guidelines for the Treatment of Eating Disorders. *Australian and New Zealand Journal of Psychiatry*, 48(11), 977–1008.

Hilbert, A., Hoek, H. W., & Schmidt, R. (2017). Evidence-based clinical guidelines for eating disorders: International comparison. *Current Opinion in Psychiatry*, 30(6), 423–437.

13 Hilbert, A., Hoek, H. W., & Schmidt, R. (2017). Evidence-based clinical guidelines for eating disorders: International comparison. *Current Opinion in Psychiatry*, 30(6), 423–437.

14 National Institute for Health and Care Excellence (NICE) (2017). *Eating Disorders: Recognition and Treatment* (NICE Guideline 143). www.nice.org.uk/guidance/ng69 (accessed on 19 December 2022).

15 Fairburn, C. G. (2008). *Cognitive Behaviour Therapy and Eating Disorders*. New York: Guilford Press.

16 National Institute for Health and Care Excellence (NICE) (2017). *Eating Disorders: Recognition and Treatment* (NICE Guideline 143). www.nice.org.uk/guidance/ng69 (accessed on 19 December 2022).

17 Zeeck, A., Herpertz-Dahlmann, B., Friederich, H. C., Brockmeyer, T., *et al.* (2018). Psychotherapeutic treatment for anorexia nervosa: A systematic review and network meta-analysis. *Frontiers in Psychiatry*, 9, 158.

18 Hilbert, A., Petroff, D., Herpertz, S., Pietrowsky, R., *et al.* (2019). Meta-analysis of the efficacy of psychological and medical

treatments for binge-eating disorder. *Journal of Consulting and Clinical Psychology, 87*(1), 91–105.

19 Eddy, K. T., Tabri, N., Thomas, J. J., Murray, H. B., *et al.* (2017). Recovery from anorexia nervosa and bulimia nervosa at 22-year follow-up. *Journal of Clinical Psychiatry, 78*(2), 184–189.

20 Smink, F. R., Van Hoeken, D., & Hoek, H. W. (2012). Epidemiology of eating disorders: Incidence, prevalence and mortality rates. *Current Psychiatry Reports, 14*(4), 406–414.

21 Vall, E., & Wade, T. D. (2015). Predictors of treatment outcome in individuals with eating disorders: A systematic review and meta-analysis. *International Journal of Eating Disorders, 48*(7), 946–971.

22 Vall, E., & Wade, T. D. (2015). Predictors of treatment outcome in individuals with eating disorders: A systematic review and meta-analysis. *International Journal of Eating Disorders, 48*(7), 946–971.

23 British Psychological Society (2013). *Classification of Behaviour and Experience in Relation to Functional Psychiatric Diagnoses: Time for a Paradigm Shift. DCP Position Statement.* Leicester: British Psychological Society.

24 Mitrofan, O., Petkova, H., Janssens, A., Kelly, J., *et al.* (2019). Care experiences of young people with eating disorders and their parents: Qualitative study. *BJPsych Open, 5*(1), e6.

25 Wufong, E., Rhodes, P., & Conti, J. (2019). 'We don't really know what else we can do': Parent experiences when adolescent distress persists after the Maudsley and family-based therapies for anorexia nervosa. *Journal of Eating Disorders, 7*(1), 1–18.

26 Tchanturia, K., Smith, K., Glennon, D., & Burhouse, A. (2020). Towards an improved understanding of the anorexia nervosa and autism spectrum comorbidity: PEACE pathway implementation. *Frontiers in Psychiatry, 11*, 640.

27 Russell, J., Mulvey, B., Bennett, H., Donnelly, B., & Frig, E. (2019). Harm minimization in severe and enduring anorexia nervosa. *International Review of Psychiatry, 31*(4), 391–402.

Chapter 4

1 Maharaj, N. (2001). *I Am That: Talks with Sri Nisargadatta*. New Delhi: Aperture. p. 1.

2 Merleau-Ponty, M., & Smith, C. (1962). *Phenomenology of Perception* (vol. 26). London: Routledge.

3 Merleau-Ponty, M., & Smith, C. (1962). *Phenomenology of Perception* (vol. 26). London: Routledge.

4 Pirandello, L. (2018 [1925]). *One, No One, and One Hundred Thousand*. Fairhope, AL: Mockingbird Press LLC [Kindle edition].

5 Pirandello, L. (2018 [1925]). *One, No One, and One Hundred Thousand*. Fairhope, AL: Mockingbird Press LLC [Kindle edition]. Chapter 1.

6 Ghezzani, N. (2004). *Crescere in un mondo malato: Bambini e adolescenti in una società in crisi* (vol. 48). Milan: Franco Angeli.

Chapter 5

1 National Institute for Health and Care Excellence (NICE) (2019). What is the prognosis? https://cks.nice.org.uk/topics/eating-disorders/background-information/prognosis (accessed on 25 January 2023).

2 Papathomas, A., Smith, B., & Lavallee, D. (2015). Family experiences of living with an eating disorder: A narrative analysis. *Journal of Health Psychology, 20*(3), 313–325.

3 Davidson, L., O'Connell, M. J., Tindora, J., Lawless, M., & Evans, A. C. (2005). Recovery in serious mental illness: A new wine or just a new bottle? *Professional Psychology: Research and Practice, 36*(5), 480–487.

Chapter 6

1 Prochaska, J. O., & DiClemente, C. C. (1992). Stages of change in the modification of problem behaviours. *Progress in Behaviour Modification, 28,* 183–218.

2 Schore, J. R., & Schore, A. N. (2008). Modern attachment theory: The central role of affect regulation in development and treatment. *Clinical Social Work Journal, 36*(1), 9–20.

3 Aron, L. (2013). *A Meeting of Minds: Mutuality in Psychoanalysis.* London: Routledge.

4 Aron, L. (2013). *A Meeting of Minds: Mutuality in Psychoanalysis.* London: Routledge.

5 Skårderud, F. (2013). Hilde Bruch (1904–1984) – the constructive use of ignorance. *Advances in Eating Disorders, 1*(2), 174–181.

6 Papathomas, A., & Lavallee, D. (2012). Eating disorders in sport: A call for methodological diversity. *Revista de Psicología del Deporte, 21*(2), 387–392.

7 Ghezzani, N. (2017). Disturbi alimentari: Un'analisi psicologica. http://nicolaghezzani.altervista.org/psicologia_disturbi_psicologici_psicoterapia-disturbi_alimentari.html (accessed December 2018).

Nesbitt, S., & Giombini, L. (2021). *Emotion Regulation for Young People with Eating Disorders: A Guide for Professionals.* London: Routledge.

8   Miller, A. (2008). *The Drama of Being a Child: The Search for the True Self*. London: Virago.

9   Bruch, H. (2001). *The Golden Cage: The Enigma of Anorexia Nervosa*. Cambridge, MA: Harvard University Press.

10 Nesbitt, S., & Giombini, L. (2021). *Emotion Regulation for Young People with Eating Disorders: A Guide for Professionals*. London: Routledge.

11 Ghezzani, N. (2004). *Crescere in un mondo malato: Bambini e adolescenti in una società in crisi* (vol. 48). Milan: Franco Angeli.

Index